DO Drops

Volume 8

DO Drops
Volume 8

Daily Bible Devotional

Dr. Bo Wagner

Word of His Mouth Publishers
Mooresboro, NC

All Scripture quotations are taken from the **King James Version** of the Bible.

ISBN: 978-1-941039-61-8
Printed in the United States of America
©2022 Dr. Bo Wagner

Word of His Mouth Publishers
Mooresboro, NC
www.wordofhismouth.com

Cover art by Chip Nuhrah

Devotion 01

David was king, and the people were joyful. But David was just getting started. And as he did, there was one item at the very top of his agenda.

1 Chronicles 13:1 *And David consulted with the captains of thousands and hundreds, and with every leader.* **2** *And David said unto all the congregation of Israel, If it seem good unto you, and that it be of the LORD our God, let us send abroad unto our brethren every where, that are left in all the land of Israel, and with them also to the priests and Levites which are in their cities and suburbs, that they may gather themselves unto us:* **3** *And let us bring again the ark of our God to us: for we enquired not at it in the days of Saul.* **4** *And all the congregation said that they would do so: for the thing was right in the eyes of all the people.*

For around fifty to sixty years, the Ark of God had been resting in Kirjathjearim, all but forgotten. David observed that "*we enquired not at it in the days of Saul.*" Little wonder, then, that Saul's reign was such a disaster! He had access to a direct communication line with God Himself and did not avail himself of it. Right at the beginning of his reign, David determined to change that. But it is six seemingly insignificant words at the beginning of his speech that are so profound to me at this point: "*If it seem good unto you.*"

In case you have forgotten, David was the king. But rather than simply give orders, he gathered his trusted advisors together, laid out his plan, and said in so many words, "What do you think?" He had the AUTHORITY just to say, "Do what I say." But he had the WISDOM to say, "What do you say?" Little wonder, then, that no King of Israel was ever as loved and revered as David.

DO have enough wisdom to rally people to your cause rather than just rail on them and expect them to follow!

Personal Notes:

_____

_____

_____

_____

_____

_____

_____

_____

_____

_____

_____

_____

_____

_____

_____

_____

_____

_____

_____

_____

_____

_____

Devotion 02

David wanted to bring back the Ark of God; he wanted it to be the central item in all of Jewish life. There is no doubt at all that this was the right thing to do and that his motivations were pure. And David would not spare any expense in so doing:

1 Chronicles 13:5 *So David gathered all Israel together, from Shihor of Egypt even unto the entering of Hemath, to bring the ark of God from Kirjathjearim. 6 And David went up, and all Israel, to Baalah, that is, to Kirjathjearim, which belonged to Judah, to bring up thence the ark of God the LORD, that dwelleth between the cherubims, whose name is called on it. 7 And they carried the ark of God in a new cart out of the house of Abinadab: and Uzza and Ahio drave the cart.*

A new cart. "Nice touch, David! A lesser man or a greedier man would have simply picked any old cart out that was already available. God is sure to be pleased!"

Not so much. In fact, not at all.

1 Chronicles 13:9 *And when they came unto the threshingfloor of Chidon, Uzza put forth his hand to hold the ark; for the oxen stumbled. 10 And the anger of the LORD was kindled against Uzza, and he smote him, because he put his hand to the ark: and there he died before God.*

No one was ever allowed to touch the Ark. And Uzza would not have felt the need to touch the Ark if it had been carried the way God specifically told the Israelites to carry it, by staffs through the rings in the side, on the shoulders of the Levites. It was written down in the law; there was no need to miss it. So, while David's motivation was right, his failure to consult Scripture led to a man's death.

DO understand that while our motivation for everything should always be right, just having the right motivation does not mean we are actually doing right!

Personal Notes:

_____

_____

_____

_____

_____

_____

_____

_____

_____

_____

_____

_____

_____

_____

_____

_____

_____

_____

_____

_____

_____

_____

Devotion 03

David was a man after God's own heart. And yet, after the disaster trying to move the Ark of God, something is said of David that is truly shocking.

1 Chronicles 13:12 *And David was afraid of God that day, saying, How shall I bring the ark of God home to me?* **13** *So David brought not the ark home to himself to the city of David, but carried it aside into the house of Obededom the Gittite.* **14** *And the ark of God remained with the family of Obededom in his house three months. And the LORD blessed the house of Obededom, and all that he had.*

David was afraid of God. This is the same thing and the same word used of Adam when God came looking for him in the garden after his sin. David did not yet understand what he had done wrong, but he knew he had done something wrong; otherwise, things would not have ended like they did.

We should always have a reverential fear of God, but being afraid of God because of our wrongdoing is a hard and needless way to live. It is far better just to always DO right and not have to be afraid when God comes calling!

Personal Notes:

_____

_____

_____

_____

_____

_____

_____

_____

_____

_____

_____

_____

_____

_____

_____

_____

_____

_____

_____

_____

_____

_____

_____

_____

_____

_____

_____

Devotion 04

As the account of David's fledgling kingdom continues, we read of something else that we did not see during the reign of Saul.

1 Chronicles 14:1 *Now Hiram king of Tyre sent messengers to David, and timber of cedars, with masons and carpenters, to build him an house.* **2** *And David perceived that the LORD had confirmed him king over Israel, for his kingdom was lifted up on high, because of his people Israel.*

Hiram, king of the nearby nation of Tyre, established contact with David early on in his reign. They became friends and allies, and as we read here, Hiram helped supply the materials for the house of David. During the entire reign of King Saul, this kind of thing is conspicuously missing. Saul very much seemed to be a big man with a small vision, whereas David was a small man with a big vision. Saul could see no farther than his own immediate needs and desires; David had a heart and an eye for his kingdom and for the world itself. Saul gave us nothing that lasted; no Scripture, no songs, no structures. David gave us all of that and more.

People can see if all you see is you. And if all you see is you, they will not see much in you. DO have a big vision; not only does it glorify God, but it also rallies others to your cause!

Personal Notes:

Devotion 05

When the Philistines heard that Israel now had a solid king, they immediately came to war against them, trying to destroy them before they could become strong.

1 Chronicles 14:8 *And when the Philistines heard that David was anointed king over all Israel, all the Philistines went up to seek David. And David heard of it, and went out against them.* **9** *And the Philistines came and spread themselves in the valley of Rephaim.* **10** *And David enquired of God, saying, Shall I go up against the Philistines? and wilt thou deliver them into mine hand? And the LORD said unto him, Go up; for I will deliver them into thine hand.* **11** *So they came up to Baalperazim; and David smote them there. Then David said, God hath broken in upon mine enemies by mine hand like the breaking forth of waters: therefore they called the name of that place Baalperazim.* **12** *And when they had left their gods there, David gave a commandment, and they were burned with fire.*

The big takeaway from this was that David and Israel won, and the Philistines lost. But a smaller item shown to us in the text is every bit as interesting, namely that when the Philistines realized they were losing, they abandoned their "gods." They literally just ditched them as extra weight as they ran away and left them laying on the ground like Snickers wrappers and soda cans.

How rude. But how appropriate! If you have to carry your gods anyway, why wouldn't you ditch them for a little bit better "speed or gas mileage?" If you have to carry your god rather than your god carrying you, then you have the wrong god.

DO rejoice in knowing that you could not carry God if you tried, but He can carry you with ease!

Personal Notes:

_____

_____

_____

_____

_____

_____

_____

_____

_____

_____

_____

_____

_____

_____

_____

_____

_____

_____

_____

_____

_____

_____

_____

_____

_____

Devotion 06

After recording the battle against the Philistines, the text returns to David's desire to bring the Ark of God to Jerusalem. After the disastrous first attempt, which ended in the death of Uzza, David finally did enough research to figure out how to do it right.

1 Chronicles 15:1 *And David made him houses in the city of David, and prepared a place for the ark of God, and pitched for it a tent.* **2** *Then David said, None ought to carry the ark of God but the Levites: for them hath the LORD chosen to carry the ark of God, and to minister unto him for ever.*

Out of thirteen tribes (twelve land-holding tribes plus the tribe of Levi), God chose one, exactly one, and only one tribe to carry the Ark of God: the tribe of Levi. The entire disaster of Uzza could have been avoided if this one simple instruction had been heeded. They, above anyone else in the nation, knew how to handle the Ark.

Now imagine, if you will, the howls of protest if we could somehow send a contingent of our modern "social justice warriors" back into that time and setting. "How discriminatory! How dare you bigots infer that one group of people is better than any other! We will have all of you canceled!"

Aside from the flawed logic of thinking that because one person or group is set aside by God for a task, they must think they are "better than others," the fact of the matter is that God has every right to pick whom He will for what He will. He can (and has) picked men for the head of the married home, men for the office of pastor and deacon, parents to be in charge of children, the local church to be His vehicle to accomplish His Great Commission work on earth, and Israel to be the apple of His eye as far as nations go.

DO be humble enough to let God be God; He does not and will not, ever, bow to the capricious whims of social justice warriors, even those calling themselves "ministers!"

Personal Notes:

_____

_____

_____

_____

_____

_____

_____

_____

_____

_____

_____

_____

_____

_____

_____

_____

_____

_____

_____

_____

_____

Devotion 07

David now understood what needed to be done to safely bring the Ark to Jerusalem. So he gathered the Levites and then spoke to eight of them specifically.

1 Chronicles 15:11 *And David called for Zadok and Abiathar the priests, and for the Levites, for Uriel, Asaiah, and Joel, Shemaiah, and Eliel, and Amminadab,* **12** *And said unto them, Ye are the chief of the fathers of the Levites: sanctify yourselves, both ye and your brethren, that ye may bring up the ark of the LORD God of Israel unto the place that I have prepared for it.* **13** *For because ye did it not at the first, the LORD our God made a breach upon us, for that we sought him not after the due order.*

That last phrase David spoke was such a crucial one. Previously we read simply that David was "afraid of God" when Uzza died for touching the Ark. But now David understood that God is to be sought "after the due order." In other words, there is a proper way to seek Him, and nothing else will ever be acceptable.

In the early 1900s, Russia was "blessed by a religious man" named Grigory Rasputin. And how did Rasputin "seek God?" By what he called "holy passionness," which is what we would call "sleeping around with almost everybody." God was not impressed. Nor is He impressed when we choose any other fleshly, self-created means to seek Him. He will be sought and found by the instructions given in His Word, never by what we dream up on our own.

DO understand that if you really want to seek God, you will find the instructions between the covers of the book called "The Bible!"

Personal Notes:

_____

_____

_____

_____

_____

_____

_____

_____

_____

_____

_____

_____

_____

_____

_____

_____

_____

_____

_____

_____

_____

_____

_____

_____

_____

_____

_____

_____

Devotion 08

Having readied the Levites for transporting the Ark to Jerusalem, the Levites started in on their task. Interestingly, though, the parallel passage in 2 Samuel 6:13 tells us that they stopped just six steps after they started! That is not going very far before taking a break! But the reason they stopped was so that they could offer a sacrifice to God, and the reason they wanted to stop and offer a sacrifice to God was because God "helped them."

1 Chronicles 15:25 *So David, and the elders of Israel, and the captains over thousands, went to bring up the ark of the covenant of the LORD out of the house of Obededom with joy.* **26** *And it came to pass, when God helped the Levites that bare the ark of the covenant of the LORD, that they offered seven bullocks and seven rams.*

The Levites had a task to do for God: carry the Ark. While that seems simple on its face, anything done for God requires His "help!" We cannot effectively sing, preach, witness, or even live for God without His help. And because of that, even when we are laboring with all our might for the Lord, it is appropriate to stop and thank Him for the might He gives us to labor for Him.

Never forget that anything good about us comes from God before we can ever give it back to God. So DO be thankful rather than proud!

Personal Notes:

_____

_____

_____

_____

_____

_____

_____

_____

_____

_____

_____

_____

_____

_____

_____

_____

_____

_____

_____

_____

_____

_____

_____

_____

_____

_____

_____

_____

Devotion 09

When everyone realized that they were going to be successful this time in trying to bring the Ark back to Jerusalem, a celebration broke out. And it was during that celebration that God brought up an issue of clothing for our consideration.

1 Chronicles 15:27 *And David was clothed with a robe of fine linen, and all the Levites that bare the ark, and the singers, and Chenaniah the master of the song with the singers: David also had upon him an ephod of linen.*

The text specifically tells us, for some reason, that David was wearing both a linen robe and a linen ephod. The ephod was a covering for the upper body, something like a shirt would be in our day. The robe was exactly what we think of when we use the word robe. In other words, David was thoroughly, fully, modestly clothed. But someone could not see that and made an incorrect assumption from her poor vantage point.

1 Chronicles 15:29 *And it came to pass, as the ark of the covenant of the LORD came to the city of David, that Michal the daughter of Saul looking out at a window saw king David dancing and playing: and she despised him in her heart.*

We know from a parallel account in 2 Kings 6 that when David got home, Michal, his wife, accused him of being naked in front of the people. There was a great deal of bad blood between them because of how things had been handled for many years previous (mostly by men acting like brats), and it all boiled over in this one faulty assumption. Their marriage was destroyed that day, and it was destroyed needlessly.

There is a very valuable lesson for today in all of this, though. DO investigate and verify before you instigate and vilify! Asking a question before hurling an accusation may save the most precious things in your life.

Personal Notes:

_____

_____

_____

_____

_____

_____

_____

_____

_____

_____

_____

_____

_____

_____

_____

_____

_____

_____

_____

_____

_____

_____

Devotion 10

On such a joyous occasion as bringing the Ark of God to Jerusalem to settle it there, it only made sense for there to be a joyous time of worship. But what would David, a warrior, know about worship? As it turns out, plenty, for David was a worshiper well before he was a warrior.

1 Chronicles 16:7 *Then on that day David delivered first this psalm to thank the LORD into the hand of Asaph and his brethren.*

The rest of the chapter is taken up with the Psalm that David gave Asaph and the people to sing and perform on that glorious day. The contents of it can be found later in Scripture again in Psalms 96, 105, and 106. David, the best fighter that Israel ever knew, did not think it to be in any way unmanly to also sing and play instruments and worship the Lord. I have often said, "Real men sing for God." Mind you, understand that not every "real man" can carry a tune in a bucket, but every man that truly loves the Lord should not be in the least bit embarrassed to try. If the killer of Goliath was not embarrassed to lift up his voice in song and even to write songs as we see here, then why should an electrician or plumber or carpenter or an office worker or a concrete man or a factory worker or any kind of man anywhere be embarrassed to do the same?

DO worship God, men; it is not "just for ladies." It is for the mightiest men who have ever lived as well!

Personal Notes:

_____
_____
_____
_____
_____
_____
_____
_____
_____
_____
_____
_____
_____
_____
_____
_____
_____
_____
_____
_____
_____
_____
_____
_____
_____
_____
_____

Devotion 11

Back in 1 Chronicles 14, Hiram helped build King David a house. As the nation's king and with such abundant supplies and labor as Hiram provided, it was doubtless an elaborate, elegant, comfortable home.

As we arrive in 1 Chronicles 17, David is in that house, but he is thinking about a tent. Not because he wants to go camping; no, he has something much more serious in mind.

1 Chronicles 17:1 *Now it came to pass, as David sat in his house, that David said to Nathan the prophet, Lo, I dwell in an house of cedars, but the ark of the covenant of the LORD remaineth under curtains.*

Since the time of the wilderness wanderings, the Ark of the Covenant had been housed in a simple tent, part of the portable tabernacle complex of the wilderness. That had allowed the children of Israel to carry it with them wherever they went in their wanderings. But now that they were settled down in their own land and with God's choice for king on the throne, David began to wonder whether or not something more permanent might be arranged. God had not commanded anything else to be done... nor had He commanded against something else eventually being done.

In other words, this was a situation where someone merely fixated on the letter of the law would never have taken any initiative to do anything different. But though David was a careful follower of the law at this point in his life, his relationship with God went far beyond a list of dos and don'ts. And that is the kind of man it took to eventually get the ball rolling to build the first Temple where the Ark of God would be housed.

We should obey all of the dos and don'ts of Scripture, but DO make your relationship with God about far more than that! DO take the initiative to get close to Him and DO great things for Him!

Personal Notes:

_____

_____

_____

_____

_____

_____

_____

_____

_____

_____

_____

_____

_____

_____

_____

_____

_____

_____

_____

_____

Devotion 12

David had begun to speak to the prophet Nathan about building God "a house," a place for the Ark of the Covenant to reside. Nathan, though, made a very well-intentioned mistake when he did.

1 Chronicles 17:2 *Then Nathan said unto David, Do all that is in thine heart; for God is with thee.*

This was, to be plain, an assumption on Nathan's part. He just figured that since David was David, the man after God's own heart, that God would automatically be on board with whatever David wanted to do for Him. But not too long after, he found out that was not the case in this instance.

1 Chronicles 17:3 *And it came to pass the same night, that the word of God came to Nathan, saying,* **4** *Go and tell David my servant, Thus saith the LORD, Thou shalt not build me an house to dwell in:*

In the next few devotions, we will see and get into the reasons why God told David no. For now, just understand that God's will is more than just "doing right and avoiding doing wrong." His will is much deeper than a wordy list; it is a way of life.

DO avoid making assumptions about the will of God unless He has put something down in writing on the subject!

Personal Notes:

_____

_____

_____

_____

_____

_____

_____

_____

_____

_____

_____

_____

_____

_____

_____

_____

_____

_____

_____

_____

_____

_____

_____

_____

_____

_____

Devotion 13

After telling Nathan to inform David that he could not build Him a house, God began to give His reasoning for that decision. And in so doing, He informed us of something that is pretty instructive.

1 Chronicles 17:5 *For I have not dwelt in an house since the day that I brought up Israel unto this day; but have gone from tent to tent, and from one tabernacle to another.*

This verse tells us one obvious thing: the Ark of God and the presence of God moved from place to place as God had the people move from place to place. He traveled with them. But the less obvious thing that it tells us is that through the years, the contents and tabernacles themselves were replaced as they wore out. The Ark of the covenant never wore out and never had to be replaced, but the tent it was housed in did. That is a pretty good picture of the child of God, which 1 Corinthians 6:19 says is the "*temple of the Holy Ghost.*" God inside of us never ages or wears out, but our body, His "tent," does!

But just like that Old Testament tent was replaced, our tent will one day be replaced as well:

2 Corinthians 5:1 *For we know that if our earthly house of this tabernacle were dissolved, we have a building of God, an house not made with hands, eternal in the heavens.*

If you feel like your "tent" is getting threadbare and tattered, DO remember that you have a new one waiting for you!

Personal Notes:

_____

_____

_____

_____

_____

_____

_____

_____

_____

_____

_____

_____

_____

_____

_____

_____

_____

_____

_____

_____

_____

_____

_____

_____

_____

_____

_____

_____

_____

Devotion 14

God went into several verses with Nathan giving him a message to give to David. And part of that message was going to be particularly precious to him.

1 Chronicles 17:11 *And it shall come to pass, when thy days be expired that thou must go to be with thy fathers, that I will raise up thy seed after thee, which shall be of thy sons; and I will establish his kingdom.* **12** *He shall build me an house, and I will stablish his throne for ever.*

There is no doubt that David would be disappointed at not being allowed to build God a house. And yet all of that disappointment was more than washed away when he was informed that one of his sons would take the throne after him, that God would establish his kingdom and his throne forever, and that he would build God the house that David would not be allowed to build.

When a person is young and single, they tend to only think of their plans for the future, where they will live, what they will do, and what they will have. But then they grow up and get married, kids start coming along, and the funniest thing happens. Suddenly, all of those things that meant so much in earlier bygone days do not mean as much anymore. When we look into the eyes of those precious children, we want them to do better than we have done, have more than we have had, and above all, do more for God than we have ever done.

DO invest yourselves in the generations coming after you; teach them to be serving the Lord long after you are gone!

Personal Notes:

_____

_____

_____

_____

_____

_____

_____

_____

_____

_____

_____

_____

_____

_____

_____

_____

_____

_____

_____

_____

_____

_____

_____

_____

_____

Devotion 15

Nathan came and delivered the message of God to David; he would not be allowed to build God a house, but his son after him would. David, in turn, spoke the words of 1 Chronicles 17:17-27, a prayer of tribute and praise and thanksgiving to God. He spoke gloriously of God's dealings with the nation of Israel, and he praised God at length for His long legacy of mercy and grace to them.

But in all of that glowing tribute, there is one seemingly simple phrase that sticks out to me of particular importance:

1 Chronicles 17:23 *Therefore now, LORD, let the thing that thou hast spoken concerning thy servant and concerning his house be established for ever, and do as thou hast said.*

"*Do as thou hast said.*" In other words, "God, you have made the call on this, and I am not going to argue. You said you were going to do it; I am one hundred percent in line with your desires, so just go ahead and do it." That is absolutely and always the right attitude for a child of God.

DO make sure that your heart attitude is, "God, whatever you have said you are going to do, I am on board, so go ahead and do it!"

Personal Notes:

_____

_____

_____

_____

_____

_____

_____

_____

_____

_____

_____

_____

_____

_____

_____

_____

_____

_____

_____

_____

_____

_____

_____

_____

_____

_____

_____

_____

Devotion 16

1 Chronicles 18 begins to describe for us the conquests of David. He was a warrior, and under his reign, Israel achieved the heights of her glory, and her landmass was bigger than ever. And during one of those conquests, David and Israel took a very valuable prize.

1 Chronicles 18:6 *Then David put garrisons in Syriadamascus; and the Syrians became David's servants, and brought gifts. Thus the LORD preserved David whithersoever he went.* **7** *And David took the shields of gold that were on the servants of Hadarezer, and brought them to Jerusalem.*

Some years afterward, Israel herself would follow this pattern and have golden shields:

1 Kings 10:16 *And king Solomon made two hundred targets of beaten gold: six hundred shekels of gold went to one target.* **17** *And he made three hundred shields of beaten gold; three pound of gold went to one shield: and the king put them in the house of the forest of Lebanon.*

In both cases, those valuable golden shields were later taken by enemies. But rather than question why they were lost, an even better question would be why they were ever even made to begin with! A shield is a defensive weapon, and in those days had to protect the user from swords, spears, and arrows. I assume that everyone knows that gold is not exactly "vibranium." Captain America would never make a shield out of it. Gold is a very soft, malleable metal, just about the worst metal on earth to defend yourself with. And that does not even take into account the fact that it is shiny!

"Hey, Moshe, I think I'll make myself a shield. Got anything soft and shiny so I can make a shield?"

"Um, sure, but wouldn't it be easier just to go ahead and shoot yourself with about a thousand arrows rather than going all the way to the battlefield to have it done?"

DO think more of substance than of style; soft and shiny things are of no use in a physical or spiritual battle!

Personal Notes:

_____
_____
_____
_____
_____
_____
_____
_____
_____
_____
_____
_____
_____
_____
_____
_____
_____
_____
_____

Devotion 17

In 1 Chronicles 18:3, we saw that David fought and defeated the king by the name of Hadarezer. When news of that got out, David soon had some very special visitors show up on that account:

1 Chronicles 18:9 *Now when Tou king of Hamath heard how David had smitten all the host of Hadarezer king of Zobah;* **10** *He sent Hadoram his son to king David, to enquire of his welfare, and to congratulate him, because he had fought against Hadarezer, and smitten him; (for Hadarezer had war with Tou;) and with him all manner of vessels of gold and silver and brass.*

This was a case of another king and another kingdom extending kindness to David and his kingdom. And that is perhaps why David soon did the exact same thing to a different King and kingdom:

1 Chronicles 19:1 *Now it came to pass after this, that Nahash the king of the children of Ammon died, and his son reigned in his stead.* **2** *And David said, I will shew kindness unto Hanun the son of Nahash, because his father shewed kindness to me. And David sent messengers to comfort him concerning his father. So the servants of David came into the land of the children of Ammon to Hanun, to comfort him.*

But where David had graciously received the messengers from another king, when he sent messengers to King Hanun, things went very differently.

1 Chronicles 19:3 *But the princes of the children of Ammon said to Hanun, Thinkest thou that David doth honour thy father, that he hath sent comforters unto thee? are not his servants come unto thee for to search, and to overthrow, and to spy out the land?* **4** *Wherefore Hanun took David's servants, and shaved them, and cut off their garments in the midst hard by their buttocks, and sent them away.*

We will say more about this in the next devotion, but for now, just let me say DO refrain from being a jerk. It's nice to be nice, and it doesn't cost anything!

Personal Notes:

_____

_____

_____

_____

_____

_____

_____

_____

_____

_____

_____

_____

_____

_____

_____

_____

Devotion 18

David had sent his messengers on a mission of kindness to King Hanun. Hanun, in turn, humiliated those innocent men by shaving off half of their beards and baring their buttocks. And that is what makes the next two verses so utterly bewildering:

1 Chronicles 19:6 *And when the children of Ammon saw that they had made themselves odious to David, Hanun and the children of Ammon sent a thousand talents of silver to hire them chariots and horsemen out of Mesopotamia, and out of Syriamaachah, and out of Zobah. **7** So they hired thirty and two thousand chariots, and the king of Maachah and his people; who came and pitched before Medeba. And the children of Ammon gathered themselves together from their cities, and came to battle.*

The part of those two verses that is so bewildering is the little three-letter word "saw." They "saw" that they had made themselves odious to David. Does it not seem like they would have very clearly known ahead of time that that is exactly what was going to happen? How is it they were so imperceptive that we basically find them going, "Dudes, you are not going to believe this; David is mad at us for what we did!"

That is some leftist politician-level unawareness.

DO have enough sense not to miss the obvious. Obvious things are obvious for a reason, and we shouldn't be surprised at them!

Personal Notes:

_____
_____
_____
_____
_____
_____
_____
_____
_____
_____
_____
_____
_____
_____
_____
_____
_____
_____
_____
_____
_____
_____
_____
_____
_____
_____
_____

Devotion 19

Israel and the Ammonites were now going to war over what King Hanun did to David's messengers. The Ammonites had hired help, and Joab, who was in charge of Israel's forces, knew that it was not going to be an easy battle. And in the words that he spoke, we find a rare and instructive moment of godliness from this man who turned out to be so very wicked.

1 Chronicles 19:10 *Now when Joab saw that the battle was set against him before and behind, he chose out of all the choice of Israel, and put them in array against the Syrians.* **11** *And the rest of the people he delivered unto the hand of Abishai his brother, and they set themselves in array against the children of Ammon.* **12** *And he said, If the Syrians be too strong for me, then thou shalt help me: but if the children of Ammon be too strong for thee, then I will help thee.* **13** *Be of good courage, and let us behave ourselves valiantly for our people, and for the cities of our God: and let the LORD do that which is good in his sight.*

In Joab's closing words, we find the predictable rallying cry for everyone to be brave and to fight for all that they were worth. But we also find him closing his pep talk with the words "*and let the LORD do that which is good in his sight.*" In other words, Joab understood that he and everyone else were responsible for giving their absolute best effort, but that at the end of the day, the results were still up to God.

DO understand the Biblical balance that we are to have in our lives: every day, in everything, we are to try as if everything depends on us, and we are to trust as if everything depends on God!

Personal Notes:

_____

_____

_____

_____

_____

_____

_____

_____

_____

_____

_____

_____

_____

_____

_____

_____

_____

_____

_____

_____

_____

_____

_____

_____

_____

Devotion 20

The battle was joined, and it was a hot one. Multiple nations, multiple kings, multiple fields. But in the end, we read this:

1 Chronicles 19:18 *But the Syrians fled before Israel; and David slew of the Syrians seven thousand men which fought in chariots, and forty thousand footmen, and killed Shophach the captain of the host.* **19** *And when the servants of Hadarezer saw that they were put to the worse before Israel, they made peace with David, and became his servants: neither would the Syrians help the children of Ammon any more.*

That last phrase, *"neither would the Syrians help the children of Ammon any more,"* is a pretty interesting statement. They lost 47,000 men in the battle and determined that the Ammonites had gotten them into more trouble than it was ever worth. And they reasoned that if they had gotten them into that depth of trouble once, they would most certainly do it again. Because of that, they were wise enough to never again "answer the phone when the caller ID said 'Ammon.'"

It would be wonderful if every Christian, young or old, could grasp this concept. Yet wicked people seem to be a magnet that some Christians are drawn to over and over again, no matter how much trouble they get them into. DO have enough sense if a person has gotten you into trouble once, to never let it happen again. To paraphrase the old statement,

"Fool me once, shame on you, fool me twice, then apparently my mama raised a fool!"

Personal Notes:

_____
_____
_____
_____
_____
_____
_____
_____
_____
_____
_____
_____
_____
_____
_____
_____
_____
_____
_____
_____
_____
_____
_____
_____
_____
_____
_____
_____

Devotion 21

The text for our consideration today is noteworthy not just for what it says but also for what it does not say.

1 Chronicles 20:1 *And it came to pass, that after the year was expired, at the time that kings go out to battle, Joab led forth the power of the army, and wasted the country of the children of Ammon, and came and besieged Rabbah. But David tarried at Jerusalem. And Joab smote Rabbah, and destroyed it.* **2** *And David took the crown of their king from off his head, and found it to weigh a talent of gold, and there were precious stones in it; and it was set upon David's head: and he brought also exceeding much spoil out of the city.*

This sequence of events is also recorded for us in 2 Samuel 11. But as you likely know, there is a rather significant event in that passage that is completely omitted in this passage, namely David committing adultery with Bathsheba and then murdering her husband, Uriah. With such a significant event, why would the writer of 2 Samuel include it but the writer of 1 Chronicles omit it? We know that all Scripture is inspired, and that certainly is enough explanation for us, but there is also something else we should consider. The books of 1 and 2 Samuel, according to the Jews, were written primarily by Samuel and then finished off by Gad and Nathan. In other words, it was written right in the days when it happened. But 1 Chronicles was written by Ezra hundreds of years later... hundreds of years

AFTER David repented. So, when God inspired this book, He left out the sin that David had so long ago repented of.

DO rejoice in knowing that because Christ died for all mankind, God chooses to forget the sins of those who repent before Him!

Personal Notes:

_____

_____

_____

_____

_____

_____

_____

_____

_____

_____

_____

_____

_____

_____

_____

_____

_____

_____

_____

_____

_____

_____

_____

_____

_____

Devotion 22

Continuing the account of King David's conquests against his enemies, we come now to some very large men from a very familiar background...

1 Chronicles 20:4 *And it came to pass after this, that there arose war at Gezer with the Philistines; at which time Sibbechai the Hushathite slew Sippai, that was of the children of the giant: and they were subdued.* **5** *And there was war again with the Philistines; and Elhanan the son of Jair slew Lahmi the brother of Goliath the Gittite, whose spear staff was like a weaver's beam.* **6** *And yet again there was war at Gath, where was a man of great stature, whose fingers and toes were four and twenty, six on each hand, and six on each foot: and he also was the son of the giant.* **7** *But when he defied Israel, Jonathan the son of Shimea David's brother slew him.* **8** *These were born unto the giant in Gath; and they fell by the hand of David, and by the hand of his servants.*

These Philistine giants, mostly from the family of Goliath himself, had been a problem to Israel for years. But have you ever stopped to consider the fact that Israel never once had any of her own "giants" to match up against them? Those on God's side were always just average men, but those on the devil's side were often actual giants. And yet God's side never lost against any of them. The family of Goliath went down time and time again against God-empowered men half their size.

If you want to be big but lose, be on the devil's side. But if you want to be small and simply win time and time again in God's power, DO be on the Lord's side!

Personal Notes:

_____

_____

_____

_____

_____

_____

_____

_____

_____

_____

_____

_____

_____

_____

_____

_____

_____

_____

_____

_____

_____

_____

_____

_____

_____

_____

_____

_____

_____

_____

Devotion 23

1 Chronicles 21:1 *And Satan stood up against Israel, and provoked David to number Israel.*

2 Samuel 24 and 1 Chronicles 21 record what appears to be one of the last official acts of David, and it was not a good one. Both of these chapters record the day when David numbered the people of Israel, something God had very clearly made known that He did not want done at that time.

Having disobeyed, David quickly realized that he was once again in trouble. And yet, when God sent word to him with the options for his punishment, the choice of David is a very instructive one for us.

2 Samuel 24:11 *For when David was up in the morning, the word of the LORD came unto the prophet Gad, David's seer, saying,* **12** *Go and say unto David, Thus saith the LORD, I offer thee three things; choose thee one of them, that I may do it unto thee.* **13** *So Gad came to David, and told him, and said unto him, Shall seven years of famine come unto thee in thy land? or wilt thou flee three months before thine enemies, while they pursue thee? or that there be three days' pestilence in thy land? now advise, and see what answer I shall return to him that sent me.* **14** *And David said unto Gad, I am in a great strait: let us fall now into the hand of the LORD; for his mercies are great: and let me not fall into the hand of man.*

Notice very carefully what David said: "*let US fall now into the hand of the LORD; for his mercies are great: and let ME not fall into the hand of man.*" In the options that God offered, option number two would fall primarily on David, while options one and three would fall on everyone. David chose one of the options that would fall on everyone, not just on himself. This was the king looking out for the king...

How very different is our great King, the Lord Jesus Christ! Our King took all of our punishment on Himself so that we may go free and be saved. DO honor the King; there has never been another His equal!

Personal Notes:

_____

_____

_____

_____

_____

_____

_____

_____

_____

_____

_____

_____

_____

_____

_____

_____

_____

_____

_____

_____

Devotion 24

A great many people died because of David's sin and stubbornness. But at the very end of the judgment, we find a most unique scene playing out.

1 Chronicles 21:16 *And David lifted up his eyes, and saw the angel of the LORD stand between the earth and the heaven, having a drawn sword in his hand stretched out over Jerusalem. Then David and the elders of Israel, who were clothed in sackcloth, fell upon their faces.* **17** *And David said unto God, Is it not I that commanded the people to be numbered? even I it is that have sinned and done evil indeed; but as for these sheep, what have they done? let thine hand, I pray thee, O LORD my God, be on me, and on my father's house; but not on thy people, that they should be plagued.*

This was not a dream or a vision; this was God peeling back the veil between the seen and the unseen world and letting David and everyone with him see what was happening. And to David (who did not know that God had already commanded the angel to cease), it looked like Jerusalem was about to take the brunt of the judgment. And it was that fact that finally broke David and humbled him to the point of asking to take the punishment on himself instead of anyone else having to die.

Mankind fancies himself as the "top of the food chain." We make weapons that shoot and explode and cut and melt. But what good is any of that against an unseen angel with a sword that can neither be seen by the eye nor stopped by any material thing?

We would do well to develop quite a bit more humility before God. An intangible Spirit who made all tangible things out of literally nothing is not intimidated by any of the material things we make out of His material.

DO be humble!

Personal Notes:

_____

_____

_____

_____

_____

_____

_____

_____

_____

_____

_____

_____

_____

_____

_____

_____

_____

_____

_____

_____

_____

_____

_____

_____

_____

Devotion 25

David had begged God for the plague to stop. And God was going to answer, telling David what he needed to do next.

1 Chronicles 21:18 *Then the angel of the LORD commanded Gad to say to David, that David should go up, and set up an altar unto the LORD in the threshingfloor of Ornan the Jebusite.* **19** *And David went up at the saying of Gad, which he spake in the name of the LORD.* **20** *And Ornan turned back, and saw the angel; and his four sons with him hid themselves. Now Ornan was threshing wheat.*

Ornan is, to me, a rather interesting character. People are dying all around... and Ornan is threshing wheat. His sons are hiding in fear... and Ornan is threshing wheat. An angel is standing over him with a sword... and Ornan is threshing wheat. Ornan did not stop what he was doing until David, the king, showed up to speak to him!

1 Chronicles 21:21 *And as David came to Ornan, Ornan looked and saw David, and went out of the threshingfloor, and bowed himself to David with his face to the ground.*

Ornan's philosophy of life seems to have been, "Today I am either going to live or die. If I live, I don't want to be behind on my work. If I die, I don't want to have left any work undone."

I like this guy.

DO have enough character and composure to stay at the work when others are hiding in fear; God's work is a great work and worthy of great efforts!

Personal Notes:

Devotion 26

When Ornan went out to meet David, a business transaction quickly took place. And by our standards today, it was one of the oddest business deals in history.

1 Chronicles 21:22 *Then David said to Ornan, Grant me the place of this threshingfloor, that I may build an altar therein unto the LORD: thou shalt grant it me for the full price: that the plague may be stayed from the people. **23** And Ornan said unto David, Take it to thee, and let my lord the king do that which is good in his eyes: lo, I give thee the oxen also for burnt offerings, and the threshing instruments for wood, and the wheat for the meat offering; I give it all. **24** And king David said to Ornan, Nay; but I will verily buy it for the full price: for I will not take that which is thine for the LORD, nor offer burnt offerings without cost. **25** So David gave to Ornan for the place six hundred shekels of gold by weight.*

David: "I want to buy your property for full price so that I can give it away."

Ornan: "Nope, I will just give it all to you for free so that you can give it away."

David: "Thanks, but I insist on paying top dollar, not a penny less."

How many business deals have you ever heard go that way? But you see, since the LORD was going to be the recipient, both men were willing to do anything and everything for Him. And when people have that heart attitude, beautiful, unusual things happen.

DO have an attitude that says, "Anything for Jesus!"

Personal Notes:

_____
_____
_____
_____
_____
_____
_____
_____
_____
_____
_____
_____
_____
_____
_____
_____
_____
_____
_____
_____
_____
_____
_____
_____
_____

Devotion 27

The judgment was over, and Ornan had sold David the parcel of property that God directed David to set up an altar on. But the next few verses give us one more eye-opening bit of information.

1 Chronicles 21:27 *And the Lord commanded the angel; and he put up his sword again into the sheath thereof.* **28** *At that time when David saw that the Lord had answered him in the threshingfloor of Ornan the Jebusite, then he sacrificed there.* **29** *For the tabernacle of the Lord, which Moses made in the wilderness, and the altar of the burnt offering, were at that season in the high place at Gibeon.* **30** *But David could not go before it to enquire of God: for he was afraid because of the sword of the angel of the Lord.*

Under normal circumstances, David would have gone to wherever the Ark of God was to get counsel from God on what to do. But his sin brought judgment and destruction, and he was now afraid to even speak to God.

That is a bad place to get to and entirely unnecessary. DO live your life so fully for the Lord that you know His hand will always be a welcoming hand rather than a chastening hand!

Personal Notes:

Devotion 28

David, always a man of passion in any purpose, was now a man on a mission unlike any other he had ever undertaken.

1 Chronicles 22:2 *And David commanded to gather together the strangers that were in the land of Israel; and he set masons to hew wrought stones to build the house of God. 3 And David prepared iron in abundance for the nails for the doors of the gates, and for the joinings; and brass in abundance without weight; 4 Also cedar trees in abundance: for the Zidonians and they of Tyre brought much cedar wood to David.*

This would be the most important construction project in the nation's history. David would not have the honor of doing it himself, but that did not stop him from doing everything he could to make it easier for the one who would have that honor.

1 Chronicles 22:5 *And David said, Solomon my son is young and tender, and the house that is to be builded for the LORD must be exceeding magnifical, of fame and of glory throughout all countries: I will therefore now make preparation for it. So David prepared abundantly before his death.*

That last phrase is so poignant and powerful; *David prepared abundantly before his death.*

If you have the ability to read these words, then you already know that you are dying. Maybe not today, maybe not next week or next year, but sometime. So what should we do about this unfortunate reality? The exact same thing that David did; prepare abundantly for those who will come after us.

DO make abundant preparations to ensure that those who come after you continue on in the service of the Lord that you hopefully have spent your life in!

Personal Notes:

_____
_____
_____
_____
_____
_____
_____
_____
_____
_____
_____
_____
_____
_____
_____
_____
_____
_____
_____
_____
_____
_____
_____
_____
_____
_____

Devotion 29

David finally pulled his son Solomon aside and told him what was on his heart concerning the house of God.

1 Chronicles 22:11 *Now, my son, the LORD be with thee; and prosper thou, and build the house of the LORD thy God, as he hath said of thee.* **12** *Only the LORD give thee wisdom and understanding, and give thee charge concerning Israel, that thou mayest keep the law of the LORD thy God.* **13** *Then shalt thou prosper, if thou takest heed to fulfil the statutes and judgments which the LORD charged Moses with concerning Israel: be strong, and of good courage; dread not, nor be dismayed.* **14** *Now, behold, in my trouble I have prepared for the house of the LORD an hundred thousand talents of gold, and a thousand thousand talents of silver; and of brass and iron without weight; for it is in abundance: timber also and stone have I prepared; and thou mayest add thereto.*

I am interested in all of the commands that David gave Solomon. But I am utterly fascinated by a descriptive phrase that David used in verse fourteen. He said, *"in my trouble I have prepared for the house of the LORD..."*

Yes, David's "trouble" was self-inflicted. But that does not change the significance of what he said; in fact, it only increases it! David had all kinds of reasons to simply throw in the towel and quit serving God, including the reason that often convinces people to do so, guilt. But instead, he pinned his ears back, lowered his shoulders, and plowed into the work with a passion. Because he refused to let his failures stop him from serving God, his son had an easy time building the most magnificent temple earth would ever know.

DO serve God with power and passion even "in your trouble!"

Personal Notes:

_____

_____

_____

_____

_____

_____

_____

_____

_____

_____

_____

_____

_____

_____

_____

_____

_____

_____

_____

_____

_____

_____

_____

_____

Devotion 30

As David continued instructing Solomon on the building of the temple, he uttered a phrase that I absolutely adore.

1 Chronicles 22:15 *Moreover there are workmen with thee in abundance, hewers and workers of stone and timber, and all manner of cunning men for every manner of work. **16** Of the gold, the silver, and the brass, and the iron, there is no number. Arise therefore, and be doing, and the LORD be with thee.*

"*Arise therefore, and be doing.*" Everyone loves the last phrase of that verse, "*and the LORD be with thee,*" but it is really nothing more than a flowery platitude unless we "*arise therefore, and be doing!*"

Frederick Douglass spent most of his life as a slave, and during that time, he came to know Christ as his Savior. He prayed fervently that Christ would deliver him from his slavery. In fact, he prayed that prayer for twenty years. And then one day he simply made plans and ran away...

He later said, "I prayed for twenty years, and I finally started praying with my feet!"

That is not a lack of faith; it is an acknowledgment that in everything that matters, we are not JUST to have faith; we are also to "*arise therefore and be doing!*"

Do you have something important to do today or at some later point in your life? DO arise and be DOing!

Personal Notes:

_____
_____
_____
_____
_____
_____
_____
_____
_____
_____
_____
_____
_____
_____
_____
_____
_____
_____
_____
_____
_____
_____
_____
_____
_____
_____
_____

Devotion 31

David had one last group of people to command and one last command to give concerning the building of the future temple under the hand of his son, Solomon.

1 Chronicles 22:17 *David also commanded all the princes of Israel to help Solomon his son, saying,* **18** *Is not the LORD your God with you? and hath he not given you rest on every side? for he hath given the inhabitants of the land into mine hand; and the land is subdued before the LORD, and before his people.* **19** *Now set your heart and your soul to seek the LORD your God; arise therefore, and build ye the sanctuary of the LORD God, to bring the ark of the covenant of the LORD, and the holy vessels of God, into the house that is to be built to the name of the LORD.*

David had prepared the material for the work. He had prepared the man for the work, Solomon, his son. Now he prepared the manpower for the work, getting everyone who mattered on board to help in the project. David had enough wisdom to understand that one man and a pile of material would forever be nothing more than an expensive junkyard unless many hands joined in the work.

If we are ever going to do anything great for God, we need both hands and both feet and every mouth belonging to everyone in the church family. We need every posterior in its place in the pew. We need every heart beating together for the things of the Lord. We need every mind thinking of how to forward the work. Great things for God do not happen by accident; they happen by a coordinated effort.

DO be fully engaged in that coordinated effort!

Personal Notes:

_____

_____

_____

_____

_____

_____

_____

_____

_____

_____

_____

_____

_____

_____

_____

_____

_____

_____

_____

_____

_____

_____

_____

_____

_____

_____

_____

Devotion 32

No longer the young warrior, nor even the middle-aged king at the height of his power, David was now old and knew that death was nigh. But in those last few days and weeks of his life, David set things in motion that would benefit his people for more than a thousand years.

1 Chronicles 23:1 *So when David was old and full of days, he made Solomon his son king over Israel.* **2** *And he gathered together all the princes of Israel, with the priests and the Levites.* **3** *Now the Levites were numbered from the age of thirty years and upward: and their number by their polls, man by man, was thirty and eight thousand.* **4** *Of which, twenty and four thousand were to set forward the work of the house of the LORD; and six thousand were officers and judges:* **5** *Moreover four thousand were porters; and four thousand praised the LORD with the instruments which I made, said David, to praise therewith.*

Knowing that the tabernacle of God would now have a permanent home, something on a much grander scale than the simple tent of the wilderness wanderings, David gathered the Levites together, 38,000 of them, and set them in various offices to minister in the coming temple. He divided them into twenty-four courses, as the rest of the chapter shows, and the structure he set in place was still being used even in the days of Christ.

This was planning and foresight on the grandest of scales. Most people's plans never even last to the end of their own lives, much less a thousand years beyond it. But if we are ever going to give that kind of planning to anything, should it not be to the worship and service of the Lord?

There is nothing wrong with making financial plans and familial plans and educational plans, and even long-term care plans. But DO also give attention to the much more important plans; DO lay plans for your family and for your people to be worshiping and serving the Lord long beyond you!

Personal Notes:

_____
_____
_____
_____
_____
_____
_____
_____
_____
_____
_____
_____
_____
_____
_____
_____
_____
_____
_____
_____

Devotion 33

The text of 1 Chronicles continues with the description of the plans for the future that David made before he died. And as we enter into chapter twenty-five, we find within them a helpful bit of instruction for our day.

1 Chronicles 25:1 *Moreover David and the captains of the host separated to the service of the sons of Asaph, and of Heman, and of Jeduthun, who should prophesy with harps, with psalteries, and with cymbals: and the number of the workmen according to their service was: **2** Of the sons of Asaph; Zaccur, and Joseph, and Nethaniah, and Asarelah, the sons of Asaph under the hands of Asaph, which prophesied according to the order of the king. **3** Of Jeduthun: the sons of Jeduthun; Gedaliah, and Zeri, and Jeshaiah, Hashabiah, and Mattithiah, six, under the hands of their father Jeduthun, who prophesied with a harp, to give thanks and to praise the LORD.*

These verses concern the music that would be present in the coming temple. But a rather unique phrase we should pay attention to in that context is *"who should prophesy with harps, with psalteries, and with cymbals."* Do you notice the unusual combination? It was a combination of both prophesying and music, or as we would put it, "preaching and music put together." This was a great indication that the music of the house of God was to be much more than just a catchy tune; it was to have some "theological meat" to it.

To put it plainly, much Christian music in our day gives a lot of attention to the music, beat, and performance but little to no attention to the message. If music attracts your flesh but does not change your life and increase your understanding of God and Biblical truth, it may be many things, but it is not godly.

DO realize the power of music, and DO make sure that the music you listen to makes you much more inclined to bow than to "boogie!"

Personal Notes:

_____

_____

_____

_____

_____

_____

_____

_____

_____

_____

_____

_____

_____

_____

_____

_____

_____

_____

_____

_____

Devotion 34

As the chapters of 1 Chronicles continue with their description of the preparations that David made for the service of the house of God before he died, we arrive in chapter twenty-six and find a new part of that preparation.

1 Chronicles 26:1 *Concerning the divisions of the porters: Of the Korhites was Meshelemiah the son of Kore, of the sons of Asaph.*

A porter was a gatekeeper, a person charged, among other tasks, with the task of keeping everyone inside safe. And it is for that reason, we find a descriptive phrase concerning some of them just a few verses later.

1 Chronicles 26:7 *The sons of Shemaiah; Othni, and Rephael, and Obed, Elzabad, whose brethren were strong men, Elihu, and Semachiah.* **8** *All these of the sons of Obededom: they and their sons and their brethren, able men for strength for the service, were threescore and two of Obededom.* **9** *And Meshelemiah had sons and brethren, strong men, eighteen.*

Strong men, verse seven. Strength for the service, verse eight. Strong men, verse nine. Do you see the trend? These were men that you would not want to mess with. These were men who could fight. These were men with power. These were men that the modern world would try their best to feminize, proclaiming them to be examples of "toxic masculinity."

In other words, they were exactly what we ought to be trying to raise our own sons to be, and they are exactly the kind of men we should be looking for as spouses for our daughters. Yes, I understand quite well that this is of less importance than spirituality. Clearly, that must always come first. But we ought to raise our boys to be strong both spiritually and physically and to be ready to do combat in either of those arenas.

DO thank God for strong men, and DO raise your sons to be such!

Personal Notes:

_____

_____

_____

_____

_____

_____

_____

_____

_____

_____

_____

_____

_____

_____

_____

_____

_____

_____

_____

Devotion 35

As the text of 1 Chronicles continues with David's preparation for the house of God, a new aspect of service is given, one that should be familiar still in our day.

1 Chronicles 26:24 *And Shebuel the son of Gershom, the son of Moses, was ruler of the treasures.* **25** *And his brethren by Eliezer; Rehabiah his son, and Jeshaiah his son, and Joram his son, and Zichri his son, and Shelomith his son.* **26** *Which Shelomith and his brethren were over all the treasures of the dedicated things, which David the king, and the chief fathers, the captains over thousands and hundreds, and the captains of the host, had dedicated.* **27** *Out of the spoils won in battles did they dedicate to maintain the house of the LORD.*

In verse twenty-four, we found the word treasures, we found it again in verse twenty-six, and in verse twenty-seven, we find that those treasures were dedicated to maintaining the house of the Lord. People had given specifically to the upkeep of the house of God and the work that went on within it.

Churches do a great deal of "reaching out." They send missionaries, feed the hungry, and tend to the poor. But they also need to be maintained, or they will cease to exist, and all of that "reaching out" will cease to exist along with them. People today still have churches to go to because other people have been giving to those works for longer than many others have even been alive.

DO maintain the house of God and the work that goes on within it!

Personal Notes:

_____

_____

_____

_____

_____

_____

_____

_____

_____

_____

_____

_____

_____

_____

_____

_____

_____

_____

_____

_____

_____

_____

_____

_____

_____

_____

_____

_____

Devotion 36

We now arrive at a verse in the text that sadly often gets skimmed over when it should be causing people to slam on the brakes and look again very carefully.

1 Chronicles 26:28 *And all that Samuel the seer, and Saul the son of Kish, and Abner the son of Ner, and Joab the son of Zeruiah, had dedicated; and whosoever had dedicated any thing, it was under the hand of Shelomith, and of his brethren.*

The subject at hand is still the fact that people had given generously to the work of the Lord. But two of the names on this list ought to jump out at us as truly shocking, namely Saul and Joab. Saul was the first king of Israel and the man who tried to murder David at least twelve different times. Joab was the long-time general of David's armies and also the man who murdered both noble Abner and David's son Absalom. And yet both of them have their names listed here for the good that they did toward the house of God.

That one will likely make us gulp just a bit. The standard operating procedure of our day is to erase people from the records and even from memory if they do something wrong. But that isn't the way it was done in David's day. As uncomfortable as it makes us, we still should not pretend that people who did wrong did not, at some points, also do right. We should simply be honest about both.

DO be honest, both about the good and the bad concerning everyone!

Personal Notes:

_____

_____

_____

_____

_____

_____

_____

_____

_____

_____

_____

_____

_____

_____

_____

_____

_____

_____

_____

_____

_____

_____

_____

_____

_____

_____

_____

_____

Devotion 37

As the account of David's choice servants begins to be wrapped up, we find something very special and heartwarming in the list.

1 Chronicles 27:32 *Also Jonathan David's uncle was a counsellor, a wise man, and a scribe: and Jehiel the son of Hachmoni was with the king's sons:* **33** *And Ahithophel was the king's counsellor: and Hushai the Archite was the king's companion:* **34** *And after Ahithophel was Jehoiada the son of Benaiah, and Abiathar: and the general of the king's army was Joab.*

In this list, we find counselors, men of great wisdom, and impeccable advice. We find warriors. We find priests. We even find the general of the army. And then we find one man who reminds me a lot of the old Sesame Street song, "one of these things is not like the other, one of these things is not the same…"

The end of verse thirty-three says, "And Hushai the Archite was the king's companion." The word companion simply means "friend." Let that one sink in. In amongst the list of warriors and priests and generals, we find a friend...

David had once had a friend, a very good friend named Jonathan. But after the death of Jonathan, we do not find many references to people who were simply friends of David. We find a loyal man, great warriors, people that meant a lot to David. I am not minimizing any of that. But the simple companionship of Hushai was so significant to David that it was recorded forever in the Word of God.

There is something incredibly powerful about just being a true friend. In a world where everyone seems to have ulterior motives, a genuine friend who does not have anything else in mind is worth his or her weight in gold.

You may not be able to do much else, but if you can be a true friend to someone, you have done something that even God thought was significant enough to record forever in Scripture. DO be a true friend!

Personal Notes:

_____

_____

_____

_____

_____

_____

_____

_____

_____

_____

_____

_____

_____

_____

_____

_____

_____

_____

_____

Devotion 38

David had a great assemblage of people in front of him, and they were all very important people:

1 Chronicles 28:1 *And David assembled all the princes of Israel, the princes of the tribes, and the captains of the companies that ministered to the king by course, and the captains over the thousands, and captains over the hundreds, and the stewards over all the substance and possession of the king, and of his sons, with the officers, and with the mighty men, and with all the valiant men, unto Jerusalem. 2 Then David the king stood up upon his feet, and said, Hear me, my brethren, and my people...*

All of these important people that were standing before David would have been willing to listen to him if he had simply sat on his throne and uttered a speech. And no one would have blamed him for doing so; David was, by this point, very old and very weak. But verse two tells us that before he uttered a word, he made the laborious effort to stand up on his feet. What topic could be so important to compel a weak old man to stand anyway? We do not have to guess; the text tells us.

1 Chronicles 28:2 *...As for me, I had in mine heart to build an house of rest for the ark of the covenant of the LORD, and for the footstool of our God, and had made ready for the building:*

The subject on David's heart was that of the house of God. It was so important to him that he struggled to his feet before he would even speak of it in front of the people. What a radical difference from how most people regard the house of God today! And yet, because of his passion for the house of God, a glorious temple came into existence and stood for half a millennia and millions of worshipers poured in and out of it for all of that time.

There will never be any substitute for the house of God, so DO be just as passionate about it as David was!

Personal Notes:

_____

_____

_____

_____

_____

_____

_____

_____

_____

_____

_____

_____

_____

_____

_____

_____

_____

_____

_____

_____

_____

_____

_____

Devotion 39

David was passionate about the house of God – and yet he would not be the one who was allowed to build it.

1 Chronicles 28:3 *But God said unto me, Thou shalt not build an house for my name, because thou hast been a man of war, and hast shed blood.* **4** *Howbeit the LORD God of Israel chose me before all the house of my father to be king over Israel for ever: for he hath chosen Judah to be the ruler; and of the house of Judah, the house of my father; and among the sons of my father he liked me to make me king over all Israel:* **5** *And of all my sons, (for the LORD hath given me many sons,) he hath chosen Solomon my son to sit upon the throne of the kingdom of the LORD over Israel.* **6** *And he said unto me, Solomon thy son, he shall build my house and my courts: for I have chosen him to be my son, and I will be his father.*

In verse four, David said that God had "chosen" him over all of his brothers to be king and that He had chosen Judah over all the other tribes to be the ruling tribe. Then in verse five, he said that God had chosen Solomon to be king after him. Then he pointed out in verse six that it was God's choice for Solomon to build the house of God instead of him.

God certainly did a whole lot of choosing, didn't He! And yet He has every right to do so; without Him, none of us would even exist. Furthermore, those choices lead to a prosperous kingdom for everyone and a glorious temple for everyone to worship in. So the next time you feel like

God has slighted you by not choosing you for one thing or the other, DO remember that just like the choices He made with David and Judah and Solomon, everyone ultimately benefits from those choices!

Personal Notes:

_____

_____

_____

_____

_____

_____

_____

_____

_____

_____

_____

_____

_____

_____

_____

_____

_____

_____

_____

_____

_____

_____

_____

_____

_____

_____

Devotion 40

Having pointed out that God had chosen Solomon to build the temple, David then turned his attention to the people and to Solomon and addressed them both. And as he did, he brought up a whole lot of "ifs."

1 Chronicles 28:7 *Moreover I will establish his kingdom for ever, IF he be constant to do my commandments and my judgments, as at this day.* **8** *Now therefore in the sight of all Israel the congregation of the LORD, and in the audience of our God, keep and seek for all the commandments of the LORD your God: that ye may possess this good land, and leave it for an inheritance for your children after you for ever.* **9** *And thou, Solomon my son, know thou the God of thy father, and serve him with a perfect heart and with a willing mind: for the LORD searcheth all hearts, and understandeth all the imaginations of the thoughts: IF thou seek him, he will be found of thee; but IF thou forsake him, he will cast thee off for ever.* **10** *Take heed now; for the LORD hath chosen thee to build an house for the sanctuary: be strong, and do it.*

Notice that God made very strong promises to Solomon, but they were conditional promises. They all hinged on those "ifs."

Some of the promises that God makes us are unconditional, wholly un-dependent on us. But most of His promises, especially promises concerning blessings and favor in this life are very, very conditional on our continued obedience. Salvation is completely by grace through faith, but blessings are largely by obedience! DO right in all of the "ifs!"

Personal Notes:

_____

_____

_____

_____

_____

_____

_____

_____

_____

_____

_____

_____

_____

_____

_____

_____

_____

_____

_____

_____

_____

_____

_____

_____

_____

_____

_____

_____

_____

Devotion 41

David had commissioned and commanded Solomon, his son, to build a house of the Lord. But he did not just command it; he gave Solomon the one thing (other than supplies) that he would most need to do it—a blueprint.

1 Chronicles 28:11 *Then David gave to Solomon his son the pattern of the porch, and of the houses thereof, and of the treasuries thereof, and of the upper chambers thereof, and of the inner parlours thereof, and of the place of the mercy seat,* **12** *And the pattern of all that he had by the spirit, of the courts of the house of the LORD, and of all the chambers round about, of the treasuries of the house of God, and of the treasuries of the dedicated things:* **13** *Also for the courses of the priests and the Levites, and for all the work of the service of the house of the LORD, and for all the vessels of service in the house of the LORD.*

Solomon did not have to guess what the temple would be like; his father provided both the material and the blueprints that he would need. David would never live to see the beginning of the temple, much less the completion of it. But his careful planning made his son successful in the venture.

Living a life is good; it certainly beats the alternative. Living a life for God is excellent; it certainly beats just living a life. But living a life for God and then handing that blueprint down to your children so that they can live a life for God is the best alternative by far. How successful can we really consider ourselves if we never handed down a pattern for our children to follow?

DO make your life a blueprint for your children to follow to God and His will after you are gone!

Personal Notes:

_____

_____

_____

_____

_____

_____

_____

_____

_____

_____

_____

_____

_____

_____

_____

_____

_____

_____

_____

_____

_____

_____

_____

_____

_____

_____

Devotion 42

As David continued to hand the blueprints for the temple to Solomon, his son, 1 Chronicles 28:12-18 tells us that even the construction of the candlesticks and vessels for the temple were preplanned and pre-supplied. This set of blueprints would have rivaled or surpassed the intricate detail of anything in our modern world. But where did David get all of these minute details? We do not have to guess; he told us quite plainly.

1 Chronicles 28:19 *All this, said David, the LORD made me understand in writing by his hand upon me, even all the works of this pattern.*

"*In writing, by His hand upon me...*" In other words, God breathed out the words to David, and David put them down on parchment. That is what the New Testament calls "inspiration."

2 Timothy 3:16 *All scripture is given by inspiration of God...*

This is so important. You need to understand, everyone needs to understand, that the Bible is not a book authored by men; men were merely the penmen. There is no book like the Bible. There has never been, and there never will be. So DO revere the sixty-six inspired books that God has preserved for us even to our very day!

Personal Notes:

_____

_____

_____

_____

_____

_____

_____

_____

_____

_____

_____

_____

_____

_____

_____

_____

_____

_____

_____

_____

_____

_____

_____

_____

_____

Devotion 43

To say that David had big dreams for the temple of God would be an understatement. But what he envisioned his son Solomon building after him was going to take more than dreams; it was going to take financial backing. And, as he did in almost everything, David led by example before asking anyone else to do anything.

1 Chronicles 29:1 *Furthermore David the king said unto all the congregation, Solomon my son, whom alone God hath chosen, is yet young and tender, and the work is great: for the palace is not for man, but for the LORD God.* **2** *Now I have prepared with all my might for the house of my God the gold for things to be made of gold, and the silver for things of silver, and the brass for things of brass, the iron for things of iron, and wood for things of wood; onyx stones, and stones to be set, glistering stones, and of divers colours, and all manner of precious stones, and marble stones in abundance.* **3** *Moreover, because I have set my affection to the house of my God, I have of mine own proper good, of gold and silver, which I have given to the house of my God, over and above all that I have prepared for the holy house,* **4** *Even three thousand talents of gold, of the gold of Ophir, and seven thousand talents of refined silver, to overlay the walls of the houses withal:* **5** *The gold for things of gold, and the silver for things of silver, and for all manner of work to be made by the hands of artificers. And who then is willing to consecrate his service this day unto the LORD?*

David led by example, and only then did he ask others to follow. And that led to a predictable result:

1 Chronicles 29:6 *Then the chief of the fathers and princes of the tribes of Israel, and the captains of thousands and of hundreds, with the rulers of the king's work, offered willingly,*

The list of what they gave is extravagant; they followed David's example well. And the point of all this is much bigger than money or church. It actually applies to everything. If we have expectations of others, the best starting point for getting those others to fulfill our expectations is for us to do so first! The old "do as I say, not as I do" paradigm is a recipe for failure, not for success.

If you want people to follow, DO walk the path yourself ahead of them!

Personal Notes:

_____

_____

_____

_____

_____

_____

_____

_____

_____

_____

_____

_____

_____

Devotion 44

When David saw what the people had so freely given, he began to rejoice and pray out loud at the same time. And it is in that prayer of rejoicing that we find an essential piece of doctrine that all of us should understand.

1 Chronicles 29:10 *Wherefore David blessed the LORD before all the congregation: and David said, Blessed be thou, LORD God of Israel our father, for ever and ever.* **11** *Thine, O LORD, is the greatness, and the power, and the glory, and the victory, and the majesty: for all that is in the heaven and in the earth is thine; thine is the kingdom, O LORD, and thou art exalted as head above all.* **12** *Both riches and honour come of thee, and thou reignest over all; and in thine hand is power and might; and in thine hand it is to make great, and to give strength unto all.* **13** *Now, therefore, our God, we thank thee, and praise thy glorious name.* **14** *But who am I, and what is my people, that we should be able to offer so willingly after this sort? for all things come of thee, and of thine own have we given thee.*

"*All that is in the heaven and in the earth is thine... all things come of thee, and of thine own have we given thee...*"

David understood that no one ever gives anything to God that God did not first give to them! If you are able to give one hundred dollars to the work of the Lord or one hundred trillion dollars to the work of the Lord, it is because He gave it to you, to begin with. We are living in His universe; every bit of matter and energy within it literally belongs to Him!

Don't just give; give and give Him the glory. DO remember where all of it came from to begin with!

Personal Notes:

_____

_____

_____

_____

_____

_____

_____

_____

_____

_____

_____

_____

_____

_____

_____

_____

_____

_____

_____

_____

_____

_____

Devotion 45

As David continued to pray and to praise, he used a word that is both beautiful and surprising, the word "imagination."

1 Chronicles 29:15 *For we are strangers before thee, and sojourners, as were all our fathers: our days on the earth are as a shadow, and there is none abiding. **16** O LORD our God, all this store that we have prepared to build thee an house for thine holy name cometh of thine hand, and is all thine own. **17** I know also, my God, that thou triest the heart, and hast pleasure in uprightness. As for me, in the uprightness of mine heart I have willingly offered all these things: and now have I seen with joy thy people, which are present here, to offer willingly unto thee. **18** O LORD God of Abraham, Isaac, and of Israel, our fathers, keep this for ever in the imagination of the thoughts of the heart of thy people, and prepare their heart unto thee:*

Notice that David used the words "imagination" and "thoughts" in near proximity. In other words, they are not the same thing. There are thoughts, and then there are, as David observed, "*the imagination of the thoughts of the heart.*" In other words, thoughts can be just random facts and figures bouncing around in our heads; imaginations are gigantic dreams and plans and hopes. David knew that if the temple was ever actually to come into being, and if it was to stand the test of time and do so gloriously, it would have to captivate the imagination of the people.

DO join together with others in the body to have gigantic dreams and plans and hopes, "imaginations" of a great house of God and great things happening for a very long time within it!

Personal Notes:

_____
_____
_____
_____
_____
_____
_____
_____
_____
_____
_____
_____
_____
_____
_____
_____
_____
_____
_____
_____
_____
_____
_____
_____
_____
_____
_____

Devotion 46

David was bringing the ceremony to a close and, in fact, was also saying some of the very last words he would ever say. He was old and dying, and he knew it.

1 Chronicles 29:20 *And David said to all the congregation, Now bless the LORD your God. And all the congregation blessed the LORD God of their fathers, and bowed down their heads, and worshipped the LORD, and the king.* **21** *And they sacrificed sacrifices unto the LORD, and offered burnt offerings unto the LORD, on the morrow after that day, even a thousand bullocks, a thousand rams, and a thousand lambs, with their drink offerings, and sacrifices in abundance for all Israel:* **22** *And did eat and drink before the LORD on that day with great gladness. And they made Solomon the son of David king the second time, and anointed him unto the LORD to be the chief governor, and Zadok to be priest.*

David's work was done, and he ended it by once again instructing his people to bless, to praise the Lord their God. David did a lot of that...

And all of that makes sense. But as we arrive at verse twenty-two, something is said that may not make sense unless you remember the account of David and Solomon from the book of 1 Kings. We are told in verse twenty-two that on that day, Solomon was anointed as king for a second time. Why was he anointed as king more than once? Because a bit earlier, his brother Adonijah, seeing that David was dying, tried to take the throne for himself. David had

Solomon hastily anointed as king to put down the rebellion. But now we find all of the people taking place in a nationwide ceremony to anoint Solomon as king. You see, there is great power in ceremony. No, "pomp and circumstance" are never THE most important thing, but they are AN important thing.

DO participate in and enjoy proper pomp and circumstance!

Personal Notes:

_____

_____

_____

_____

_____

_____

_____

_____

_____

_____

_____

_____

_____

_____

_____

_____

_____

_____

_____

_____

_____

_____

Devotion 47

The life and reign of David were now at an end. Here is how it was summarized for us at the end of 1 Chronicles.

1 Chronicles 29:26 *Thus David the son of Jesse reigned over all Israel.* **27** *And the time that he reigned over Israel was forty years; seven years reigned he in Hebron, and thirty and three years reigned he in Jerusalem.* **28** *And he died in a good old age, full of days, riches, and honour: and Solomon his son reigned in his stead.* **29** *Now the acts of David the king, first and last, behold, they are written in the book of Samuel the seer, and in the book of Nathan the prophet, and in the book of Gad the seer,* **30** *With all his reign and his might, and the times that went over him, and over Israel, and over all the kingdoms of the countries.*

He reigned for forty years. He lived to a ripe old age, accomplished almost everything he set his heart to, achieved glory that no king before or after him would even come near to, and lived long enough to see his son established on the throne after him. David's life was a complex mixture of the heroic and the occasionally heinous, principal and sometimes pettiness, wisdom and the odd, "What was he thinking?" kind of moment.

In other words, he was an actual human being who loved the Lord but didn't always get things right. And yet God used him mightily anyway.

DO make up your mind to always do right. But don't despair and quit when you fail. DO exactly what David always did—repent, get back up, brush yourself off, and get right back to serving God like you should!

Personal Notes:

_____
_____
_____
_____
_____
_____
_____
_____
_____
_____
_____
_____
_____
_____
_____
_____
_____
_____
_____
_____
_____
_____
_____
_____
_____
_____
_____
_____

Devotion 48

David was now dead, and Solomon, his son, was firmly established on the throne. David had given great thought to the things of God, and Solomon would continue that and even expand upon it.

2 Chronicles 1:2 *Then Solomon spake unto all Israel, to the captains of thousands and of hundreds, and to the judges, and to every governor in all Israel, the chief of the fathers. 3 So Solomon, and all the congregation with him, went to the high place that was at Gibeon; for there was the tabernacle of the congregation of God, which Moses the servant of the LORD had made in the wilderness. 4 But the ark of God had David brought up from Kirjathjearim to the place which David had prepared for it: for he had pitched a tent for it at Jerusalem. 5 Moreover the brasen altar, that Bezaleel the son of Uri, the son of Hur, had made, he put before the tabernacle of the LORD: and Solomon and the congregation sought unto it. 6 And Solomon went up thither to the brasen altar before the LORD, which was at the tabernacle of the congregation, and offered a thousand burnt offerings upon it.*

During his reign, David had been fixated on one particular item in the tabernacle of God, the Ark of the Covenant. And while that was an excellent fixation, it was also a narrow fixation. There were more items of worship that God had commanded to be used in the tabernacle. David had taken that one item and moved it to a tent in Jerusalem, regarding it as more important than all the rest. But while it was, the rest were still important! So Solomon began to turn his attention to "the forgotten things" of worship, things like the tabernacle itself and the brazen altar within the tabernacle.

It is easy to get fixated on just one part of worship, be it attending or preaching or praying or singing or giving or witnessing, or any other part of worship. And while all of those are good things, the wisest course we can take is to always give attendance to everything having to do with the worship of God. So rather than focusing just on one thing, DO make sure you don't miss anything!

Personal Notes:

_____

_____

_____

_____

_____

_____

_____

_____

_____

_____

_____

_____

_____

_____

_____

_____

_____

_____

_____

Devotion 49

After reading of Solomon seeking out the tabernacle and the altar, we find recorded for us in 2 Chronicles 1 the account which was previously given in 1 Kings 3 of God handing a blank check to Solomon. Solomon asked for wisdom, and God granted it to him along with that which he had not asked for, incredible wealth. And then, the text begins to describe a bit of that great wealth:

2 Chronicles 1:14 *And Solomon gathered chariots and horsemen: and he had a thousand and four hundred chariots, and twelve thousand horsemen, which he placed in the chariot cities, and with the king at Jerusalem.* **15** *And the king made silver and gold at Jerusalem as plenteous as stones, and cedar trees made he as the sycomore trees that are in the vale for abundance.* **16** *And Solomon had horses brought out of Egypt, and linen yarn: the king's merchants received the linen yarn at a price.* **17** *And they fetched up, and brought forth out of Egypt a chariot for six hundred shekels of silver, and an horse for an hundred and fifty: and so brought they out horses for all the kings of the Hittites, and for the kings of Syria, by their means.*

What is described here is utterly staggering wealth, and it does not even begin to exhaust the list of Solomon's wealth given in the furtherance of Scripture. And it was very specifically God Himself that gave it. But before you look at that and then compare it to your day-by-day life of perhaps living from paycheck to paycheck, do remember that these material blessings of God on his life are actually nowhere near as great as the blessings that God has given you! You have things that Solomon did not have, things like a completed Bible, the indwelling Holy Spirit, and the full knowledge of Christ and Calvary and the resurrection. The poorest believer in this age is infinitely better off than the wealthiest believer in Old Testament times.

DO remember that for believers, "the good old days" are actually right now!

Personal Notes:

_____

_____

_____

_____

_____

_____

_____

_____

_____

_____

_____

_____

_____

_____

_____

_____

_____

_____

_____

_____

Devotion 50

David had spent many years preparing the precious materials such as gold and silver, and now Solomon was going to begin the actual construction of the glorious temple of God. And one of the first things he did was prepare for the manpower that would be needed for the task.

2 Chronicles 2:1 *And Solomon determined to build an house for the name of the LORD, and an house for his kingdom.* **2** *And Solomon told out threescore and ten thousand men to bear burdens, and fourscore thousand to hew in the mountain, and three thousand and six hundred to oversee them.*

As you can see from the numbers, there were 150,000 laborers preparing in gathering the materials. We also find listed here 3,600 supervisors. In the account of this from 1 Kings 5, we find a bit of a different number, 3,300. The reason for the difference is that the account of 1 Kings gives us only "the chief of Solomon's officers" which amounted to 3,300, and the account in 2 Chronicles also gives us the additional 300 supervisors who were not of the chief of Solomon's officers.

But no matter which number you are looking at, one thing that is very evident is that there were far more "workers" than there were "bosses." Both were needed, but the workers were needed more by approximately a fifty-to-one ratio.

Have you ever had those days where you felt like little more than an ant in a colony? DO keep in mind that the wisest man who ever lived so very much understood the necessity and value of common workers that he appointed them at nearly a fifty-to-one rate over supervisors!

Personal Notes:

_____

_____

_____

_____

_____

_____

_____

_____

_____

_____

_____

_____

_____

_____

_____

_____

_____

_____

_____

_____

_____

_____

_____

_____

_____

_____

_____

_____

Devotion 51

As David, his father, had done before him, Solomon now reached out to an ally to the north, Hiram (here spelled Huram), king of Tyre, asking for help building the temple. There was a genuine friendship between these kings and these kingdoms, and Hiram was glad to help. In fact, as he wrote to Solomon agreeing to help, he informed Solomon that he had just the man to oversee the project from his side. And the information he gave about this man, while often simply glossed over, actually ought to have people slamming on the brakes to stop and take a closer look.

2 Chronicles 2:11 *Then Huram the king of Tyre answered in writing, which he sent to Solomon, Because the LORD hath loved his people, he hath made thee king over them.* **12** *Huram said moreover, Blessed be the LORD God of Israel, that made heaven and earth, who hath given to David the king a wise son, endued with prudence and understanding, that might build an house for the LORD, and an house for his kingdom.* **13** *And now I have sent a cunning man, endued with understanding, of Huram my father's,* **14** *The son of a woman of the daughters of Dan, and his father was a man of Tyre, skilful to work in gold, and in silver, in brass, in iron, in stone, and in timber, in purple, in blue, and in fine linen, and in crimson; also to grave any manner of graving, and to find out every device which shall be put to him, with thy cunning men, and with the cunning men of my lord David thy father.*

"The son of a woman of the daughters of Dan, and his father was a man of Tyre..."

This man, ladies and gentlemen, who was going to have such a crucial role in building the house of God, was half Jew and half Gentile. There is almost no way to overstate the magnitude of that fact. John Wesley observed that this was "A good omen of uniting Jew and Gentile in the gospel-temple."

Even that far back, and even in something so sacred as the Temple of God, God was bringing Gentiles into the process and in very significant ways.

DO remember that God does not have so much as a racist molecule in his DNA, and neither should we!

Personal Notes:

_____

_____

_____

_____

_____

_____

_____

_____

_____

_____

_____

_____

_____

_____

_____

_____

_____

Devotion 52

The laborers for the Temple were in place, and the materials for the Temple were provided. Now would begin the actual construction. But every construction needs one more thing: a location! And that was provided as well. And, as you might expect, that location had some heavyweight significance to it.

2 Chronicles 3:1 *Then Solomon began to build the house of the LORD at Jerusalem in mount Moriah, where the LORD appeared unto David his father, in the place that David had prepared in the threshingfloor of Ornan the Jebusite. 2 And he began to build in the second day of the second month, in the fourth year of his reign.*

Moriah. That name only appears twice in Scripture; here and way back in Genesis 22.

Genesis 22:2 *And he said, Take now thy son, thine only son Isaac, whom thou lovest, and get thee into the land of Moriah; and offer him there for a burnt offering upon one of the mountains which I will tell thee of.*

In Genesis 22, we find Moriah as the place where a father, Abraham, was about to willingly sacrifice his son on the mountain. In 2 Chronicles 3, we are given a reminder that it was the place where a sacrifice was made that stopped the judgment of God. And now a temple would be set on that very mountain where lambs would be sacrificed for the sins of the people. And then one day, nearly a thousand years later, on that same mountain just outside of town, another Father would send his Son up the hill to die, another sacrifice would be made that would stop the judgment of God, and another Lamb, the last Lamb ever needed, would be slain.

Kinda gives you the idea that God knows exactly what He's doing, doesn't it!

DO remember that God never does anything "on the fly;" as Acts 15:18 says, *"Known unto God are all his works from the beginning of the world*!"

Personal Notes:

_____

_____

_____

_____

_____

_____

_____

_____

_____

_____

_____

_____

_____

_____

_____

_____

_____

_____

_____

_____

_____

_____

_____

_____

Devotion 53

As the details unfold in the text concerning the building of the temple, we are given much information about sizes and dimensions, about silver and gold overlays, about jewels and carvings. But in the midst of all that, we find what almost appears to be an oddity; two specific pieces of the temple were actually given names.

2 Chronicles 3:17 *And he reared up the pillars before the temple, one on the right hand, and the other on the left; and called the name of that on the right hand Jachin, and the name of that on the left Boaz.*

As Spurgeon observed, "These were vast columns intended for glory and for beauty." These were no simple little posts; they were massive and glorious. And one of them was named Jachin, while the other was named Boaz. And lest you forget, these names were not man's idea. Every bit of this was God's idea. David said in **1 Chronicles 28:19** *"All this, the LORD made me understand in writing by his hand upon me, even all the works of this pattern."* So it was God Himself that chose to have those pillars which would stand for nearly half a millennium named after those two men.

And one of those names you remember quite well. Boaz was the man who was willing to marry a woman and raise up a child who would bear the name of her dead husband rather than him because that is the way God wanted it. And that man who was willing to make that sacrifice was so precious to God that God immortalized his name at the very entrance of the temple of God!

DO remember that any sacrifice you make for the Lord is noticed by Him, and He has the most glorious ways of saying "thank you!"

Personal Notes:

_____

_____

_____

_____

_____

_____

_____

_____

_____

_____

_____

_____

_____

_____

_____

_____

_____

_____

_____

_____

_____

_____

_____

_____

_____

_____

Devotion 54

After describing some of the glory of the newly constructed temple itself, 2 Chronicles 4 begins to tell us of some of the furniture and furnishings within the temple. And one of those items was absolutely jaw-dropping.

2 Chronicles 4:2 *Also he made a molten sea of ten cubits from brim to brim, round in compass, and five cubits the height thereof; and a line of thirty cubits did compass it round about. 3 And under it was the similitude of oxen, which did compass it round about: ten in a cubit, compassing the sea round about. Two rows of oxen were cast, when it was cast. 4 It stood upon twelve oxen, three looking toward the north, and three looking toward the west, and three looking toward the south, and three looking toward the east: and the sea was set above upon them, and all their hinder parts were inward. 5 And the thickness of it was an handbreadth, and the brim of it like the work of the brim of a cup, with flowers of lilies; and it received and held three thousand baths.*

What is described here is a brass water container large enough to qualify as an in-ground swimming pool. It held approximately ten thousand gallons of water if filled to the brim! But this molten sea, as it was called, was not for pleasure. It was for the priests and their ceremonial cleansing before they offered sacrifice on behalf of the people.

Everything in the tabernacle and the temple was symbolic, including this. And if the priests themselves were so much in need of cleansing, how much more were the people in need of cleansing? And this went on day after day, month after month, year after year, for centuries. But our high priest, Jesus, needed no cleansing! Hebrews 10:12 says, *"But this man, after he had offered one sacrifice for sins for ever, sat down on the right hand of God."*

If you are saved, then DO rest in the assurance that salvation is secured because of His cleanliness, not yours!

Personal Notes:

_____

_____

_____

_____

_____

_____

_____

_____

_____

_____

_____

_____

_____

_____

_____

_____

_____

_____

_____

_____

_____

Devotion 55

All of the instruments for the temple were not just religious pieces of furniture, they were also amazing works of art. And the methodology by which they were made is both ancient and yet still current.

2 Chronicles 4:17 *In the plain of Jordan did the king cast them, in the clay ground between Succoth and Zeredathah.*

The casting process is still used in jewelry production today. It involves making a life-size mold of something, normally out of wax, and then immersing it into a substance that will harden around it, with a hole in the bottom that the wax can then be melted out of. The precious metal is then poured into the empty space, and the hardened substance is broken from around it. Today we normally use something like Plaster of Paris, but in those days, clay was the medium of choice.

And there was a piece of ground perfect for that, In the plain of Jordan between Succoth and Zeredathah. This clay ground, not very good at all for growing things, was perfect for casting purposes.

Often, we, people literally made from dirt, look around at others and wish we had their gifts, their talents, their abilities. But God designs each of us just the way He wants us for His glory and His purposes. You may not be quite the same dirt as someone else, but DO realize that God made you just the kind of "dirt" that He wanted you!

Personal Notes:

Devotion 56

Everything tangible was finally finished, and now there was just one thing left to do.

2 Chronicles 5:1 *Thus all the work that Solomon made for the house of the LORD was finished: and Solomon brought in all the things that David his father had dedicated; and the silver, and the gold, and all the instruments, put he among the treasures of the house of God.* **2** *Then Solomon assembled the elders of Israel, and all the heads of the tribes, the chief of the fathers of the children of Israel, unto Jerusalem, to bring up the ark of the covenant of the LORD out of the city of David, which is Zion.* **3** *Wherefore all the men of Israel assembled themselves unto the king in the feast which was in the seventh month.* **4** *And all the elders of Israel came; and the Levites took up the ark.* **5** *And they brought up the ark, and the tabernacle of the congregation, and all the holy vessels that were in the tabernacle, these did the priests and the Levites bring up.*

The Tabernacle was in Gibeon, the Ark of the Covenant was in a tent in a portion of Jerusalem called Zion, the city of David, and the new temple was sitting atop Mount Moriah. In other words, everything and therefore everyone was scattered out! So Solomon finally gathered everything into the new temple, and therefore everyone could come and worship completely together.

And it has always been God's expressed desire for his people to do so. The moment they came out of Egypt He arranged the entire nation literally

116

around His tabernacle with it in the dead center of everyone and everything. He allowed Solomon and then Zerubbabel and then Herod, of all people, to build temples for everyone to come and worship together. And then He started the local church, the ekklesia, a "called out assembly," for His people to come together and worship in. And this should tell us that anyone espousing the belief that actually going to church and worshiping together with God's people is not necessary has no idea what they are talking about...

DO pay attention to the fact that God has forever established physical places for His people to come together as an entire body and worship Him!

Personal Notes:

_____

_____

_____

_____

_____

_____

_____

_____

_____

_____

_____

_____

_____

_____

_____

_____

_____

Devotion 57

There were some glorious things in the temple, but there was one thing that far exceeded them all. In fact, everything around it was ultimately built for it.

2 Chronicles 5:4 *And all the elders of Israel came; and the Levites took up the ark.* **5** *And they brought up the ark, and the tabernacle of the congregation, and all the holy vessels that were in the tabernacle, these did the priests and the Levites bring up.* **6** *Also king Solomon, and all the congregation of Israel that were assembled unto him before the ark, sacrificed sheep and oxen, which could not be told nor numbered for multitude.* **7** *And the priests brought in the ark of the covenant of the LORD unto his place, to the oracle of the house, into the most holy place, even under the wings of the cherubims:* **8** *For the cherubims spread forth their wings over the place of the ark, and the cherubims covered the ark and the staves thereof above.*

Within the most holy place of the temple, there were already ornate golden angels placed in such a way as if they were hovering above a certain spot. And yet they were absolutely meaningless until the thing that they were to be overshadowing was in place—the Ark of the Covenant. The angels were "just angels." I mean no disrespect by that at all, but the truth of the matter is that without the presence of God, they are meaningless, and we are as well. Until they had the Ark of the Covenant, the place where God's presence would reside to hover over and attend to, they may as well have been curios sitting on someone's shelf collecting dust.

DO remember that we draw our very significance from the fact that we are made by God, and from the God who made us!

Personal Notes:

_____

_____

_____

_____

_____

_____

_____

_____

_____

_____

_____

_____

_____

_____

_____

_____

_____

_____

_____

_____

_____

_____

_____

_____

_____

_____

_____

Devotion 58

With everything including the Ark of the Covenant now in place, the "worship service" began. But it did not last long, and for all the right reasons:

2 Chronicles 5:11 *And it came to pass, when the priests were come out of the holy place: (for all the priests that were present were sanctified, and did not then wait by course:* **12** *Also the Levites which were the singers, all of them of Asaph, of Heman, of Jeduthun, with their sons and their brethren, being arrayed in white linen, having cymbals and psalteries and harps, stood at the east end of the altar, and with them an hundred and twenty priests sounding with trumpets:)* **13** *It came even to pass, as the trumpeters and singers were as one, to make one sound to be heard in praising and thanking the LORD; and when they lifted up their voice with the trumpets and cymbals and instruments of musick, and praised the LORD, saying, For he is good; for his mercy endureth for ever: that then the house was filled with a cloud, even the house of the LORD;* **14** *So that the priests could not stand to minister by reason of the cloud: for the glory of the LORD had filled the house of God.*

They had their plan and program in place. But God was so pleased by what He was seeing and hearing that He completely took over the program and just filled the place with His glory. This was an incredibly rare occasion, but it was a glorious and wonderful occasion.

There is absolutely nothing wrong with knowing what we will sing and preach and say and do during a worship service. But when God chooses in a great or even a small way to interrupt the proceedings with His manifest glory, the most sensible thing for us to do is put our program aside and enjoy it!

DO unashamedly enjoy those times!

Personal Notes:

_____

_____

_____

_____

_____

_____

_____

_____

_____

_____

_____

_____

_____

_____

_____

_____

_____

_____

_____

_____

_____

_____

_____

_____

Devotion 59

The Temple was now completed, the furnishings and the Ark of the Covenant were installed, God had moved in and interrupted the worship service, and now Solomon would close things out with a message and a prayer. Here is just a little bit of that prayer and a visual description of what the people saw as Solomon prayed it.

2 Chronicles 6:13 *For Solomon had made a brasen scaffold, of five cubits long, and five cubits broad, and three cubits high, and had set it in the midst of the court: and upon it he stood, and kneeled down upon his knees before all the congregation of Israel, and spread forth his hands toward heaven,* **14** *And said, O LORD God of Israel, there is no God like thee in the heaven, nor in the earth; which keepest covenant, and shewest mercy unto thy servants, that walk before thee with all their hearts:* **15** *Thou which hast kept with thy servant David my father that which thou hast promised him; and spakest with thy mouth, and hast fulfilled it with thine hand, as it is this day.*

The most powerful man in the entire country, arguably the most powerful man in the world at that time, visibly bowed before the God of heaven and prayed aloud to Him. And he began with the words *"O LORD God of Israel, there is no God like thee in the heaven, nor in the earth..."*

We very much live in an age where the prevailing attitude is, "Look at me, there is no one like me!" But for the person who truly knows God, the attitude will always be, "Look at Him, there is no one like Him!" And if that is the attitude that people see in us, they will be drawn to the God that we say we serve. It is when people say they believe in God and serve God and yet direct the focus and attention to themselves that a lost world is repelled by that "witness," so DO be a better kind of witness!

Personal Notes:

_____

_____

_____

_____

_____

_____

_____

_____

_____

_____

_____

_____

_____

_____

_____

_____

_____

_____

_____

_____

_____

_____

_____

_____

Devotion 60

As Solomon continued praying before the eyes of all the people, he reached a point at which he repeated a word many times in just a short span. Whenever that happens in the Bible, pay attention to it. In this case, the word is "place."

2 Chronicles 6:19 *Have respect therefore to the prayer of thy servant, and to his supplication, O LORD my God, to hearken unto the cry and the prayer which thy servant prayeth before thee:* **20** *That thine eyes may be open upon this house day and night, upon the PLACE whereof thou hast said that thou wouldest put thy name there; to hearken unto the prayer which thy servant prayeth toward this PLACE.* **21** *Hearken therefore unto the supplications of thy servant, and of thy people Israel, which they shall make toward this PLACE: hear thou from thy dwelling PLACE, even from heaven; and when thou hearest, forgive.*

Solomon had already observed in verse eighteen that even the heavens are not big enough to contain God. And yet the God who is too big for the universe chooses to live in a place called heaven where His angels and saints can be with Him, and He also chooses to meet with His people here on earth in a specific, literal place. In Solomon's day, it was the new Temple, and every heart that was right with God longed for it. In our day it is the local church, and once again every heart that is right with God longs for it. And as Israel either defiled or grew unfaithful to the Temple things always went bad for the land, and as

America defiles or grows unfaithful to the church things will grow worse and worse for our land.

DO be faithful to the house of God, the most special PLACE on earth!

Personal Notes:

_____

_____

_____

_____

_____

_____

_____

_____

_____

_____

_____

_____

_____

_____

_____

_____

_____

_____

_____

_____

_____

_____

_____

_____

_____

_____

_____

_____

_____

Devotion 61

As Solomon continued praying, and as the people listened to his words, it became as much a sermon and a theology lesson as a prayer. And when Solomon got to one particular part of it there was likely an audible gasp from the crowd.

2 Chronicles 6:32 *Moreover concerning the stranger, which is not of thy people Israel, but is come from a far country for thy great name's sake, and thy mighty hand, and thy stretched out arm; if they come and pray in this house;* **33** *Then hear thou from the heavens, even from thy dwelling place, and do according to all that the stranger calleth to thee for; that all people of the earth may know thy name, and fear thee, as doth thy people Israel, and may know that this house which I have built is called by thy name.*

Everyone knew exactly what Solomon meant by "strangers." He meant Gentiles. He meant the entire rest of the world who were not descended from Abraham. He meant people of other lands, ethnicities, skin colors, and languages.

He was literally praying that they would come to know God and come to worship along with the Jews in that glorious temple, the house of God. What a thrill it should be to our hearts to realize that God wanted to include all of us! And what a convicting thought it should be to anyone who still thinks that they are more special to God than others because of their skin color, no matter what skin color that is.

DO realize that God loves and wants to save one race; the human race!

Personal Notes:

_____

_____

_____

_____

_____

_____

_____

_____

_____

_____

_____

_____

_____

_____

_____

_____

_____

_____

_____

_____

_____

_____

_____

_____

_____

_____

_____

_____

Devotion 62

As Solomon continued the prayer/sermon/theology lesson, all of which was centered around a "place," the house of God, he said something that Daniel understood and still believed and practiced five centuries later:

2 Chronicles 6:36 *If they sin against thee, (for there is no man which sinneth not,) and thou be angry with them, and deliver them over before their enemies, and they carry them away captives unto a land far off or near;* **37** *Yet if they bethink themselves in the land whither they are carried captive, and turn and pray unto thee in the land of their captivity, saying, We have sinned, we have done amiss, and have dealt wickedly;* **38** *If they return to thee with all their heart and with all their soul in the land of their captivity, whither they have carried them captives, and pray toward their land, which thou gavest unto their fathers, and toward the city which thou hast chosen, and toward the house which I have built for thy name:* **39** *Then hear thou from the heavens, even from thy dwelling place, their prayer and their supplications, and maintain their cause, and forgive thy people which have sinned against thee.*

Daniel took this literally and prayed toward Jerusalem three times a day. Both he and later Nehemiah understood that it was the sin of the people that caused them to go into captivity, and it would take repentance of that sin and the mercy of God to get them out.

Solomon said, "*there is no man which sinneth not.*" He was correct. That is not an excuse to sin; it is just an acknowledgment of fact. So when you sin, DO turn your heart back to God, your eyes back to His house, and repent so you can be restored!

Personal Notes:

_____

_____

_____

_____

_____

_____

_____

_____

_____

_____

_____

_____

_____

_____

_____

_____

_____

_____

_____

_____

_____

_____

_____

Devotion 63

As Solomon finished praying, one of the rarest things in human history happened in front of an entire nation of witnesses:

2 Chronicles 7:1 *Now when Solomon had made an end of praying, the fire came down from heaven, and consumed the burnt offering and the sacrifices; and the glory of the LORD filled the house.* **2** *And the priests could not enter into the house of the LORD, because the glory of the LORD had filled the LORD'S house.* **3** *And when all the children of Israel saw how the fire came down, and the glory of the LORD upon the house, they bowed themselves with their faces to the ground upon the pavement, and worshipped, and praised the LORD, saying, For he is good; for his mercy endureth for ever.*

This is one of only three times that God ever sent fire down from heaven to consume a sacrifice. And in this case, it resulted in everyone bowing, placing their faces on the ground, and worshiping and praising God. But the thought that intrigues me the most is that this happened three thousand years ago, meaning there was no technology or tool even in existence to fake such a thing. In other words, an entire nation full of highly intelligent people, smart enough in fact to build the most magnificent structure in the history of the ancient world, saw an indisputable miracle, a proof of God's existence and power.

God doesn't always give "proof." But He has done so enough to make believing in Him the only logical, rational choice. So DO believe!

Personal Notes:

_____

_____

_____

_____

_____

_____

_____

_____

_____

_____

_____

_____

_____

_____

_____

_____

_____

_____

_____

_____

_____

_____

_____

_____

_____

_____

_____

Devotion 64

When we say that the whole nation was involved in the celebration of the dedication of the temple, it is a literal statement, not hyperbole. Look at what is said concerning place, people, and provisions.

2 Chronicles 7:5 *And king Solomon offered a sacrifice of twenty and two thousand oxen, and an hundred and twenty thousand sheep: so the king and all the people dedicated the house of God.* **6** *And the priests waited on their offices: the Levites also with instruments of musick of the LORD, which David the king had made to praise the LORD, because his mercy endureth for ever, when David praised by their ministry; and the priests sounded trumpets before them, and all Israel stood.* **7** *Moreover Solomon hallowed the middle of the court that was before the house of the LORD: for there he offered burnt offerings, and the fat of the peace offerings, because the brasen altar which Solomon had made was not able to receive the burnt offerings, and the meat offerings, and the fat.* **8** *Also at the same time Solomon kept the feast seven days, and all Israel with him, a very great congregation, from the entering in of Hamath unto the river of Egypt.*

22,000 oxen; huge animals. 120,000 sheep; also pretty sizeable animals. These were sacrificed, and as always, the fat was burned to the Lord, but the meat was for the people to eat. Not to make light of this, but this was likely the biggest barbecue in the history of mankind! And it had to be, since the celebration took place from Hamath, the Northern border of the land, all the way to the river on the Southern border that divided Israel from Egypt. This was a seven-day, 142,000 animal, everyone-is-invited celebration.

It is good to celebrate with God's people, so DO enjoy doing so!

Personal Notes:

_____

_____

_____

_____

_____

_____

_____

_____

_____

_____

_____

_____

_____

_____

_____

_____

_____

_____

_____

_____

_____

_____

Devotion 65

One might be tempted to think that such a glorious house of worship would forever bring God's blessings on a land and people. But if Solomon ever thought that, he was going to be surprised. Because after he dismissed everyone and sent them all home, God came to Solomon with a message, and it was a sobering one.

2 Chronicles 7:17 *And as for thee, IF thou wilt walk before me, as David thy father walked, and do according to all that I have commanded thee, and shalt observe my statutes and my judgments;* **18** *Then will I stablish the throne of thy kingdom, according as I have covenanted with David thy father, saying, There shall not fail thee a man to be ruler in Israel.* **19** *BUT if ye turn away, and forsake my statutes and my commandments, which I have set before you, and shall go and serve other gods, and worship them;* **20** *Then will I pluck them up by the roots out of my land which I have given them; and this house, which I have sanctified for my name, will I cast out of my sight, and will make it to be a proverb and a byword among all nations.*

"If... but." How often have we seen this? It is such a regular occurrence in Scripture that by now it should no longer surprise us. But it perhaps was a bit surprising to Solomon to hear God say that the glorious temple, just finished and dedicated, could one day be thrown away like a piece of garbage by God Himself. And yet that is exactly what God informed Solomon of in verse twenty. His blessings would not be secured for future generations by ornamentation; it would always and only be secured by obedience.

It is good to have a nice church building, but it is ESSENTIAL to be obedient to the God that we come to that nice building to worship!

Personal Notes:

_____

_____

_____

_____

_____

_____

_____

_____

_____

_____

_____

_____

_____

_____

_____

_____

_____

_____

_____

_____

_____

_____

_____

_____

Devotion 66

For twenty years, half of his forty-year reign, Solomon was engaged primarily in building the temple of God and his own house. But Solomon did not stop building after that; all of his reign was marked by construction and architecture. And two of the cities that he is described as building bring a great big smile to my face.

2 Chronicles 8:1 *And it came to pass at the end of twenty years, wherein Solomon had built the house of the LORD, and his own house,* **2** *That the cities which Huram had restored to Solomon, Solomon built them, and caused the children of Israel to dwell there.* **3** *And Solomon went to Hamathzobah, and prevailed against it.* **4** *And he built Tadmor in the wilderness, and all the store cities, which he built in Hamath.* **5** *Also he built Bethhoron the upper, and Bethhoron the nether, fenced cities, with walls, gates, and bars;*

Bethhoron the upper and Bethhoron the nether are mentioned previous to this time in Scripture. You see, when Solomon "built" them it was really more like a renovation because someone else long ago had already built them:

1 Chronicles 7:24 *(And his daughter was Sherah, who built Bethhoron the nether, and the upper, and Uzzensherah.)*

These two cities were built by a girl. And four hundred years later they were still significant enough to capture Solomon's attention and warrant him "building" them to even greater glory. I would wager a guess that she never expected her life's work to garner that kind of attention after that length of time from that important of a person. But none of us ever really know, do we? And therefore the wisest thing any of us can do is our absolute best at all times.

DO your best, all day, every day; you know that God notices, and you don't know who else may take notice of it somewhere down the road!

Personal Notes:

_____

_____

_____

_____

_____

_____

_____

_____

_____

_____

_____

_____

_____

_____

_____

_____

_____

_____

_____

_____

_____

_____

Devotion 67

After giving several more verses describing the various construction projects of King Solomon, the text informs us of one more building project that was commissioned for a head-scratching reason...

2 Chronicles 8:11 *And Solomon brought up the daughter of Pharaoh out of the city of David unto the house that he had built for her: for he said, My wife shall not dwell in the house of David king of Israel, because the places are holy, whereunto the ark of the LORD hath come.*

Some years earlier, in a case of a classic political alliance, Solomon married the daughter of the Pharaoh of Egypt. He brought her home to Jerusalem and allowed her to live there. But then once the Ark of God had come to Jerusalem he built another house for her to get her away from "holy places." Now, stop and think about that. What business did he have even marrying a woman who "did not fit in" in holy places? If you marry someone that you have to keep away from the house of God, it seems pretty reasonable to assume that you should not have married that person to begin with!

DO be careful whom you marry; if he or she does not "fit in" with God and godliness, then he or she should not "fit in" with your plans for life!

Personal Notes:

_____

_____

_____

_____

_____

_____

_____

_____

_____

_____

_____

_____

_____

_____

_____

_____

_____

_____

_____

_____

_____

_____

_____

_____

_____

_____

_____

Devotion 68

Solomon was firmly ensconced on the throne, and it was to him that all the nation looked for guidance. And yet, there was an unseen influence from the past still holding great sway in everything that was done.

2 Chronicles 8:12 *Then Solomon offered burnt offerings unto the LORD on the altar of the LORD, which he had built before the porch,* **13** *Even after a certain rate every day, offering according to the commandment of Moses, on the sabbaths, and on the new moons, and on the solemn feasts, three times in the year, even in the feast of unleavened bread, and in the feast of weeks, and in the feast of tabernacles.* **14** *And he appointed, according to the order of David his father, the courses of the priests to their service, and the Levites to their charges, to praise and minister before the priests, as the duty of every day required: the porters also by their courses at every gate: for so had David the man of God commanded.*

David. David his father, as the first part of verse fourteen calls him. David, the man of God as the last part of verse fourteen calls him. Everything that was happening in the worship services was happening because David had organized and arranged it before he ever handed the reins of the kingdom to Solomon. And it is because of this that David in this place, rather than being called David the king, is called David the man of God. The normal way of referring to him when speaking of the kingdom of his son would have been to call him King David. But despite his disastrous sin with Bathsheba, David still spent the last measure of his strength worshiping God and organizing worship for God.

We can be called many things based on the lives we live. But DO determine above all else to worship so fully that you could truly be called a man or woman or boy or girl of God!

Personal Notes:

_____

_____

_____

_____

_____

_____

_____

_____

_____

_____

_____

_____

_____

_____

_____

_____

_____

_____

_____

_____

_____

_____

Devotion 69

We have seen that Solomon was successful in building, but we also find that he was successful in business.

2 Chronicles 8:17 *Then went Solomon to Eziongeber, and to Eloth, at the sea side in the land of Edom.* **18** *And Huram sent him by the hands of his servants ships, and servants that had knowledge of the sea; and they went with the servants of Solomon to Ophir, and took thence four hundred and fifty talents of gold, and brought them to king Solomon.*

On this particular "business trip," a joint venture between Solomon, king of Israel, and Huram, king of Tyre, went in pursuit of gold. This required sailing to the far-off land of Ophir. So in order for the venture to be successful, there had to be a crew of people who knew how to sail and another crew of people who knew how to get gold once they arrived. And because they had both sides of that covered, the venture was wildly successful. Huram provided the mariners, Solomon provided the miners or the bargainers. The men of Tyre were not known to be successful at the acquisition of gold, and the men of Israel were not known to be successful navigators of the seas. But when they learned to work together the most amazing things became possible.

And it is still that way today, especially in the work of the Lord. God has never allowed anyone to be able to do everything. But if everyone will do what they can do and work with others who will do what they cannot do, great things can be done for our Savior. So DO work together!

Personal Notes:

_____

_____

_____

_____

_____

_____

_____

_____

_____

_____

_____

_____

_____

_____

_____

_____

_____

_____

_____

_____

_____

_____

_____

_____

_____

_____

_____

_____

Devotion 70

Solomon was quickly becoming the human wonder of the world. And because of that, he ended up with a most distinguished visitor.

2 Chronicles 9:1 *And when the queen of Sheba heard of the fame of Solomon, she came to prove Solomon with hard questions at Jerusalem, with a very great company, and camels that bare spices, and gold in abundance, and precious stones: and when she was come to Solomon, she communed with him of all that was in her heart.* **2** *And Solomon told her all her questions: and there was nothing hid from Solomon which he told her not.* **3** *And when the queen of Sheba had seen the wisdom of Solomon, and the house that he had built,* **4** *And the meat of his table, and the sitting of his servants, and the attendance of his ministers, and their apparel; his cupbearers also, and their apparel; and his ascent by which he went up into the house of the LORD; there was no more spirit in her.*

The Queen of Sheba arrived with a very specific purpose in mind, to "prove" Solomon with "hard questions." In other words, she wanted to match wits with him. She had heard of his brilliance and was clearly skeptical. And in many cases where a woman matches wits with a man, we must certainly admit to the fact that she is fighting with an unarmed adversary! But in this case, this brilliant woman was utterly bested by Solomon. And verse four tells us that when she had seen his wisdom and his works and his workers and even his walkway that there was no more spirit in her. And since the word for spirit also means breath, it would not be at all unfair to say that Solomon left her breathless!

Solomon was very much as advertised. And that makes him one of the rarest of all human beings...

In a world of fakes and phonies, DO have an excellent reputation, and DO be worthy of the excellent reputation that you have!

Personal Notes:

_____
_____
_____
_____
_____
_____
_____
_____
_____
_____
_____
_____
_____
_____
_____
_____
_____
_____
_____
_____
_____

Devotion 71

God did not choose to record for us any of the hard questions that the Queen of Sheba posed to Solomon. But He did record for us her evaluation of Solomon when the testing was over.

2 Chronicles 9:5 *And she said to the king, It was a true report which I heard in mine own land of thine acts, and of thy wisdom:* **6** *Howbeit I believed not their words, until I came, and mine eyes had seen it: and, behold, the one half of the greatness of thy wisdom was not told me: for thou exceedest the fame that I heard.* **7** *Happy are thy men, and happy are these thy servants, which stand continually before thee, and hear thy wisdom.* **8** *Blessed be the LORD thy God, which delighted in thee to set thee on his throne, to be king for the LORD thy God: because thy God loved Israel, to establish them for ever, therefore made he thee king over them, to do judgment and justice.*

This is a glorious evaluation of the King of Israel by the Queen of Sheba. But I am most intrigued right now with her words "*I believed not their words until I came and mine eyes had seen it.*" Solomon should be regarded as remarkable for being as advertised, but the Queen of Sheba should be regarded as remarkable in her own right for verifying something odd that she had heard!

Can you imagine how different life would be in our day of social media if everyone took that one example from the Queen of Sheba and made it their normal practice of life?

DO be in the habit of studying before speaking; many people in our day are nearly starving to death because almost all they ever get to eat are their own words!

Personal Notes:

_____

_____

_____

_____

_____

_____

_____

_____

_____

_____

_____

_____

_____

_____

_____

_____

_____

_____

_____

_____

_____

_____

_____

_____

_____

Devotion 72

After Solomon and the Queen of Sheba matched wits, there was a cordial and generous exchange of gifts as was absolutely normal for Oriental monarchs.

2 Chronicles 9:9 *And she gave the king an hundred and twenty talents of gold, and of spices great abundance, and precious stones: neither was there any such spice as the queen of Sheba gave king Solomon. 10 And the servants also of Huram, and the servants of Solomon, which brought gold from Ophir, brought algum trees and precious stones. 11 And the king made of the algum trees terraces to the house of the LORD, and to the king's palace, and harps and psalteries for singers: and there were none such seen before in the land of Judah. 12 And king Solomon gave to the queen of Sheba all her desire, whatsoever she asked, beside that which she had brought unto the king. So she turned, and went away to her own land, she and her servants.*

Looking at the list of gifts that are here is very interesting. But looking at what is not here is, to me, just as interesting…

Did you see the part about Solomon "luring her into his bed?" No. And do you know why you did not see that? Because it is not here to be seen. And yet "Internet theologians" constantly state it as a historical fact. And the reason people state things as facts of the Bible even though those things are not in the Bible is generally that they are too lazy to study the things that actually are in the Bible. The day that you have exhausted everything Scripture has to say, feel free to try to write things into it that it does not say. But since that day will never actually come, DO refrain from elevating legend to the height of Scripture!

Personal Notes:

_____

_____

_____

_____

_____

_____

_____

_____

_____

_____

_____

_____

_____

_____

_____

_____

_____

_____

_____

_____

_____

_____

_____

_____

_____

_____

Devotion 73

Let's look at a few more verses describing Solomon and see if you can notice the common theme.

2 Chronicles 9:13 *Now the weight of gold that came to Solomon in one year was six hundred and threescore and six talents of gold;* **14** *Beside that which chapmen and merchants brought. And all the kings of Arabia and governors of the country brought gold and silver to Solomon.* **15** *And king Solomon made two hundred targets of beaten gold: six hundred shekels of beaten gold went to one target.* **16** *And three hundred shields made he of beaten gold: three hundred shekels of gold went to one shield. And the king put them in the house of the forest of Lebanon.*

If you happened to say the word "gold" then go to the head of the class...

The gold of Solomon is mentioned sixteen times in this one chapter alone. And how wealthy was this gold-hungry monarch?

2 Chronicles 9:22 *And king Solomon passed all the kings of the earth in riches and wisdom.*

He was literally the richest man on earth. And that is what makes the request of the people to Rehoboam his son so many years later such a telling thing:

2 Chronicles 10:4 *Thy father made our yoke grievous: now therefore ease thou somewhat the grievous servitude of thy father, and his heavy yoke that he put upon us, and we will serve thee.*

Solomon could have bought everything belonging to everyone in the nation many times over. And yet he taxed his people heavily. There is no way to get around that; it was absolutely avarice and greed. He enjoyed the blessings of God, and yet, it was never enough. It is not so much that he had gold; it is more like gold had him. No wonder his later years as he himself described them in the book of Ecclesiastes were so miserable!

There will never be enough wealth to make a greedy person happy, nor will there ever be enough poverty to make a generous person miserable. DO choose generosity and happiness!

Personal Notes:

_____

_____

_____

_____

_____

_____

_____

_____

_____

_____

_____

_____

_____

_____

_____

_____

_____

Devotion 74

2 Chronicles 10 is nearly word for word what we find in 2 Kings 20. And when we looked at the breakup of the kingdom in that chapter, we focused mainly on the mistakes of King Rehoboam. But in this case, let's briefly look at the mistakes made on the other side of the issue.

2 Chronicles 10:1 *And Rehoboam went to Shechem: for to Shechem were all Israel come to make him king.* **2** *And it came to pass, when Jeroboam the son of Nebat, who was in Egypt, whither he had fled from the presence of Solomon the king, heard it, that Jeroboam returned out of Egypt.* **3** *And they sent and called him. So Jeroboam and all Israel came and spake to Rehoboam, saying,* **4** *Thy father made our yoke grievous: now therefore ease thou somewhat the grievous servitude of thy father, and his heavy yoke that he put upon us, and we will serve thee.*

Twice the people used the word grievous to describe how things had been under King Solomon. But do you know what things they did not mention that had been true under King Solomon? For forty years there had been almost no war, no invasions, and everyone had enjoyed prosperity. Throughout the entire history of Israel, this is the only lengthy period of time in which all of those things can be said! This is a good reminder, therefore, that people will find a reason to complain even if they have to look through a microscope to do so.

DO choose to focus on the vast majority of your blessed life rather than on the few things that bother you. If you don't, you will end up losing many of those blessings and have many more things to bother you!

Personal Notes:

_____

_____

_____

_____

_____

_____

_____

_____

_____

_____

_____

_____

_____

_____

_____

_____

_____

_____

_____

_____

_____

_____

_____

_____

_____

_____

_____

_____

_____

_____

_____

Devotion 75

The people of Israel had come to the new king, Rehoboam, asking for an easing of their yoke. It was not an unreasonable request, nor was it asked in an inappropriate manner. Rehoboam, for his part, asked for three days to consider their request. And here is how things went during that time:

2 Chronicles 10:6 *And king Rehoboam took counsel with the old men that had stood before Solomon his father while he yet lived, saying, What counsel give ye me to return answer to this people? 7 And they spake unto him, saying, If thou be kind to this people, and please them, and speak good words to them, they will be thy servants for ever. 8 But he forsook the counsel which the old men gave him, and took counsel with the young men that were brought up with him, that stood before him.*

That may seem like an inappropriate place to stop in the text. After all, we have not yet gotten to what the young men had to say! But that is, in fact, exactly why I stopped where I did...

In verse seven we find the counsel of the old men to King Rehoboam. Logically, we would assume that the next thing we would see would be the counsel of the young men to King Rehoboam. And then we would expect him to evaluate those two different sets of counsel to see which was the wiser course. But that is not at all what we see, sadly. After the old men gave their very wise counsel in verse seven, the very next words we read are *"But he forsook the counsel which the old men gave him."* He did not even wait to hear what the young men had to say; he had already predetermined what he wanted to hear, and unless someone said that, he was not going to listen.

This is another good evidence that people, in general, are not really seeking counsel when they ask for counsel; they are seeking approval when they ask for counsel.

DO be wise enough to actually seek out wise counsel and follow it!

Personal Notes:

_____

_____

_____

_____

_____

_____

_____

_____

_____

_____

_____

_____

_____

_____

_____

_____

_____

_____

_____

_____

Devotion 76

After three days' time, the people of the land reassembled before King Rehoboam to hear his answer to their very reasonable request. Imagine their shock when they heard the new king utter these inflammatory words:

2 Chronicles 10:13 *And the king answered them roughly; and king Rehoboam forsook the counsel of the old men,* **14** *And answered them after the advice of the young men, saying, My father made your yoke heavy, but I will add thereto: my father chastised you with whips, but I will chastise you with scorpions.*

Hearing this, they responded predictably:

2 Chronicles 10:16 *And when all Israel saw that the king would not hearken unto them, the people answered the king, saying, What portion have we in David? and we have none inheritance in the son of Jesse: every man to your tents, O Israel: and now, David, see to thine own house. So all Israel went to their tents.*

David? What did David have to do with this? Simply this: David was one man, from one tribe, Judah. And he was the head of the monarchy that had only been in existence for two short generations. In other words, everyone still remembered well that this was a nation of twelve tribes that not too many years earlier had been doing quite well without even having a king. So when Rehoboam threatened them in this manner, the other tribes simply walked away and formed their own kingdom without him. Rehoboam had never done one thing for them or accomplished one thing on his own. And yet he behaved as if everyone in the kingdom was somehow beholden to him just by birthright.

DO remember that in most cases no one owes us anything. And while being a jerk is foolish enough under any circumstances, being a jerk while never having earned any respect from others is foolish to the point of being potentially fatal!

Personal Notes:

_____

_____

_____

_____

_____

_____

_____

_____

_____

_____

_____

_____

_____

_____

_____

_____

_____

_____

_____

Devotion 77

After we read of Rehoboam's foolishness and the breakup of the kingdom that it caused, we then immediately read one thing that is both sad and hilarious, and a second thing that is subtly instructive.

2 Chronicles 10:18 *Then king Rehoboam sent Hadoram that was over the tribute; and the children of Israel stoned him with stones, that he died. But king Rehoboam made speed to get him up to his chariot, to flee to Jerusalem.* **19** *And Israel rebelled against the house of David unto this day.*

Do you sometimes feel like you have a hard job? Imagine being the tax collector for Rehoboam the day after Rehoboam threatened to abuse everybody and caused the kingdom to split! Poor Hadoram; he would have been better off resigning his post and going into business as a camel dung dealer.

But in verse nineteen we read, *"And Israel rebelled against the house of David unto this day."* Unto this day? Unto what day? The answer is, until the day hundreds of years later when Ezra put pen to parchment to write the words of the book of 2 Chronicles. Rehoboam likely thought this was just a temporary spat; but as generation after generation lived and died and passed off the scene, the chasm only grew wider.

Before you blow something up, DO ask yourself whether or not you want it to still be blown up one, ten, twenty, or fifty years down the line. If not, don't blow it up to begin with!

Personal Notes:

_____

_____

_____

_____

_____

_____

_____

_____

_____

_____

_____

_____

_____

_____

_____

_____

_____

_____

_____

_____

_____

_____

_____

_____

_____

_____

_____

_____

Devotion 78

Rehoboam had lost 10/12 of his kingdom by being a jerk and running his mouth. Naturally, though, he would not just let that go. And in his mind, he had just the solution for how to fix things.

2 Chronicles 11:1 *And when Rehoboam was come to Jerusalem, he gathered of the house of Judah and Benjamin an hundred and fourscore thousand chosen men, which were warriors, to fight against Israel, that he might bring the kingdom again to Rehoboam.*

How exactly had Rehoboam lost most of his kingdom? Again, by being a jerk and running his mouth. By making threats. And what was his solution to "fix things?" His solution was to "go beat up all of the people that were mad at him for being a jerk."

Yeah, that'll fix things for sure, genius.

In the next few verses, we will find God forbidding him from going to war with what was now the northern kingdom. But for now just please focus in on how Rehoboam was intent on taking the dumbest and hardest possible course to fix things when there was, humanly speaking, a pretty easy way to solve the problem:

Apologize.

Had Rehoboam gone to the people and admitted his mistake and apologized and asked for forgiveness, the kingdom would almost certainly have been reunited that instant. But instead he, in pride, never humbled himself enough to do so.

DO learn the value of a timely apology; no one goes through life without needing to give them from time to time, and only the foolish refuse to do so.

Personal Notes:

_____

_____

_____

_____

_____

_____

_____

_____

_____

_____

_____

_____

_____

_____

_____

_____

_____

_____

_____

_____

_____

_____

_____

_____

_____

_____

_____

Devotion 79

Rehoboam's plans were to go to war against the ten tribes that split off from him due to his high-level jerkery. But God had other plans.

2 Chronicles 11:2 *But the word of the Lord came to Shemaiah the man of God, saying,* **3** *Speak unto Rehoboam the son of Solomon, king of Judah, and to all Israel in Judah and Benjamin, saying,* **4** *Thus saith the Lord, Ye shall not go up, nor fight against your brethren: return every man to his house: for this thing is done of me. And they obeyed the words of the Lord, and returned from going against Jeroboam.*

Rehoboam really wanted to do it. Yet when God told him not to, he obeyed. He simply let go of ten-twelfths of his kingdom. Imagine a president simply allowing the loss of forty-two of the fifty states! This was a huge loss, and yet Rehoboam obeyed, going against everything in the desires of his flesh to do so.

That means that as far as obedience goes, Rehoboam did better than even David and Solomon, who both had significant instances of disobedience in their lives.

When you want to obey God, obey God. When you don't want to obey God, obey God. There is absolutely nothing in the life or ministry of a Christian that will make God give us a pass on disobedience, so DO obey!

Personal   Notes:

_____
_____
_____
_____
_____
_____
_____
_____
_____
_____
_____
_____
_____
_____
_____
_____
_____
_____
_____
_____
_____
_____
_____
_____
_____
_____
_____
_____
_____

Devotion 80

The kingdom was split, and God had let Rehoboam know that he was never getting the other ten tribes back. And our human reasoning would tell us that the ten tribes in the north would form a nation far stronger than the two tribes in the South. But both this immediate text and the four-hundred-year history that followed proved otherwise:

2 Chronicles 11:5 *And Rehoboam dwelt in Jerusalem, and built cities for defence in Judah.* **6** *He built even Bethlehem, and Etam, and Tekoa,* **7** *And Bethzur, and Shoco, and Adullam,* **8** *And Gath, and Mareshah, and Ziph,* **9** *And Adoraim, and Lachish, and Azekah,* **10** *And Zorah, and Aijalon, and Hebron, which are in Judah and in Benjamin fenced cities.* **11** *And he fortified the strong holds, and put captains in them, and store of victual, and of oil and wine.* **12** *And in every several city he put shields and spears, and made them exceeding strong, having Judah and Benjamin on his side.*

Notice those words "*exceeding strong*" and "*having Judah and Benjamin on his side.*" With just two totally devoted tribes, Rehoboam turned the southern kingdom of Judah into a much stronger kingdom than the more sizable kingdom of Israel. We never do read that the ten tribes were devoted to Jeroboam; they were simply angry with Rehoboam. And anger against will never be as strong long-term as devotion toward.

DO be devoted to God and the Word of God and the house of God. Anger against sin or the world or error will only keep you faithful for a little while, but devotion will keep you faithful forever!

Personal Notes:

_____

_____

_____

_____

_____

_____

_____

_____

_____

_____

_____

_____

_____

_____

_____

_____

_____

_____

_____

_____

_____

_____

_____

_____

_____

_____

_____

Devotion 81

As we continue to read of the ever-widening separation between the new kingdom of Israel in the North and the new kingdom of Judah in the south, we find another stark instance of the two different paths they were on.

2 Chronicles 11:13 *And the priests and the Levites that were in all Israel resorted to him* [Rehoboam] *out of all their coasts.* **14** *For the Levites left their suburbs and their possession, and came to Judah and Jerusalem: for Jeroboam and his sons had cast them off from executing the priest's office unto the LORD:* **15** *And he ordained him priests for the high places, and for the devils, and for the calves which he had made.* **16** *And after them out of all the tribes of Israel such as set their hearts to seek the LORD God of Israel came to Jerusalem, to sacrifice unto the LORD God of their fathers.*

Despite his initial snotty attitude, Rehoboam at least did not go the way of Jeroboam in regard to God. Jeroboam in the north "fired" all of the priests of God and replaced them with priests to his devils and idols. And yet those same priests of God found a welcoming home in Rehoboam and the South. In fact, verse sixteen tells us that whoever had set their hearts to seek the Lord God, priest or not, came down south to Jerusalem. The North had immediately become the home of paganism and heathenism, and the South had become the home of the worship of the God of Israel.

Little wonder then that the North never had a single good and godly king at all in its entire history!

DO be a worshiper of God and a welcomer of others who worship God; the fate of a nation is ultimately decided by worship, not by warfare.

Personal Notes:

_____

_____

_____

_____

_____

_____

_____

_____

_____

_____

_____

_____

_____

_____

_____

_____

_____

_____

_____

_____

_____

_____

_____

_____

_____

Devotion 82

The last thing that we read of Rehoboam and the southern kingdom of Judah was that things were going well, and they were getting exceedingly strong because they were continuing on in the worship of Jehovah God. But then abruptly we see a warning flag in the text begin to wave...

2 Chronicles 11:17 *So they strengthened the kingdom of Judah, and made Rehoboam the son of Solomon strong, three years: for three years they walked in the way of David and Solomon.*

Three years. In other words "uh-oh..."

Not to jump too far ahead of ourselves, but look at how the next chapter starts:

2 Chronicles 12:1 *And it came to pass, when Rehoboam had established the kingdom, and had strengthened himself, he forsook the law of the LORD, and all Israel with him.*

It took three years for Rehoboam to think he had gotten the kingdom to the level of strength that he desired. And the level of strength that he desired was "strong enough to not bother with God anymore." But there will never, ever be a time when any person or nation gets that strong. And Rehoboam and the kingdom were about to learn that the hard way.

DO maintain a spirit of humility before God. People literally made from dirt should never be so vain as to imagine that they are strong enough to no longer need the God who made the dirt that they are made from!

Personal Notes:

Devotion 83

In the last three verses of 2 Chronicles 11, we find both parenting and policy issues in the life of Rehoboam.

2 Chronicles 11:21 *And Rehoboam loved Maachah the daughter of Absalom above all his wives and his concubines: (for he took eighteen wives, and threescore concubines; and begat twenty and eight sons, and threescore daughters.)* **22** *And Rehoboam made Abijah the son of Maachah the chief, to be ruler among his brethren: for he thought to make him king.* **23** *And he dealt wisely, and dispersed of all his children throughout all the countries of Judah and Benjamin, unto every fenced city: and he gave them victual in abundance. And he desired many wives.*

Rehoboam committed the same sin as Solomon, his father, in multiplying many wives to himself. Deuteronomy 17:17 had expressly forbidden this. And though his number of wives and concubines paled in comparison to that of his famous father, the number of children he is shown to have produced is actually greater. Rehoboam had twenty-eight sons and sixty daughters by his seventy-eight wives and concubines. And he then committed the additional faux pas of choosing a favored son rather than the eldest son for the throne. And in order to keep that from causing problems he shipped his kids out to different cities all over the country to keep them from conspiring against Abijah, his chosen heir.

This, verse twenty-three says, was him acting "wisely." But please understand that when the Bible uses some form of the word of wisdom, it does not always mean godly wisdom, James 3:15 is a good example of that. And in this case, it merely meant "being shrewd and calculating."

When we compare what he did with the volume of what Scripture says, it was anything but godly wisdom. Rehoboam disobeyed God, indulged his flesh, produced more children than he could possibly actually raise right, and then shipped them away before they cause too many problems.

Definitely not "Dad of the Year."

DO be careful in your production and parenting of children; each one deserves active, godly parents who are fully invested in their lives!

Personal Notes:

_____
_____
_____
_____
_____
_____
_____
_____
_____
_____
_____
_____
_____
_____
_____
_____
_____

Devotion 84

Rehoboam now believed that he was strong enough to do without God and disobey the laws of God. He would soon find out the hard way where that kind of decision leads.

2 Chronicles 12:1 *And it came to pass, when Rehoboam had established the kingdom, and had strengthened himself, he forsook the law of the LORD, and all Israel with him.* **2** *And it came to pass, that in the fifth year of king Rehoboam Shishak king of Egypt came up against Jerusalem, because they had transgressed against the LORD,* **3** *With twelve hundred chariots, and threescore thousand horsemen: and the people were without number that came with him out of Egypt; the Lubims, the Sukkiims, and the Ethiopians.* **4** *And he took the fenced cities which pertained to Judah, and came to Jerusalem.*

In verse two we find the words "*because they had transgressed against the LORD.*" All of the disaster that befell came specifically and intentionally from God because of their disobedience. And this is interesting to consider in light of the fact that throughout Scripture God used invading armies, droughts, natural disasters, diseases, and many other things to punish nations for their wrongdoing. And yet in our day if anyone even brings up the possibility that any given disaster may well be God's judgment on our land for sin, even the popular "Christian voices" in our land began to shriek at the top of their lungs at the very suggestion of such a thing.

But there is not a single verse of Scripture that informs us that God no longer deals that way. Not one. And while we should be careful never to put words in God's mouth, we should be equally as careful whenever a disaster does fall to examine our lives and our land and see if perhaps our sin has warranted it.

DO understand that the God who so often got His people's attention by great disasters in years gone by still has the right and the ability to do so today!

Personal Notes:

_____

_____

_____

_____

_____

_____

_____

_____

_____

_____

_____

_____

_____

_____

_____

_____

_____

_____

_____

_____

Devotion 85

After forty years of peace in the days of Solomon the king, just five years into the reign of Rehoboam the people were once again experiencing the horrors of war. And they were doing so because of their disobedience to God. God, though, would not let them go through that without making them aware that it was, in fact, their sin that had caused it.

2 Chronicles 12:5 *Then came Shemaiah the prophet to Rehoboam, and to the princes of Judah, that were gathered together to Jerusalem because of Shishak, and said unto them, Thus saith the LORD, Ye have forsaken me, and therefore have I also left you in the hand of Shishak. 6 Whereupon the princes of Israel and the king humbled themselves; and they said, The LORD is righteous. 7 And when the LORD saw that they humbled themselves, the word of the LORD came to Shemaiah, saying, They have humbled themselves; therefore I will not destroy them, but I will grant them some deliverance; and my wrath shall not be poured out upon Jerusalem by the hand of Shishak. 8 Nevertheless they shall be his servants; that they may know my service, and the service of the kingdoms of the countries.*

When we are dealing with people who "get right with God," we do not have the ability to see their hearts and know if they are genuine. But when Rehoboam and his princes got right with God, God noted that they had genuinely humbled themselves. It was not just words; they meant what they were saying.

And if we were writing the story, it is likely that the next thing in the text would be "and so God sent a miraculous and full deliverance to His people." But that is not what happened. God specifically allowed them to survive, but as servants to Shishak, king of Egypt. He did this specifically so that they would evaluate whether it was better to willingly serve God or to be forced into servitude before men.

That option is not too hard to figure out. DO be smart enough to evaluate what life and eternity will be like willingly serving God versus what life and eternity will be like being left under the bondage of devils and men!

Personal Notes:

_____

_____

_____

_____

_____

_____

_____

_____

_____

_____

_____

_____

_____

_____

_____

_____

_____

Devotion 86

Rehoboam and his princes had humbled themselves before God. Because of that, God was going to show them some mercy. But it is a phrase within the description of that mercy that catches my attention at this point.

2 Chronicles 12:9 *So Shishak king of Egypt came up against Jerusalem, and took away the treasures of the house of the LORD, and the treasures of the king's house; he took all: he carried away also the shields of gold which Solomon had made.* **10** *Instead of which king Rehoboam made shields of brass, and committed them to the hands of the chief of the guard, that kept the entrance of the king's house.* **11** *And when the king entered into the house of the LORD, the guard came and fetched them, and brought them again into the guard chamber.* **12** *And when he humbled himself, the wrath of the LORD turned from him, that he would not destroy him altogether: and also in Judah things went well.*

Rehoboam repented. God showed a little bit of mercy to them. And in Judah, "*things went well.*" And while that sounds good, just a couple of years earlier we find the phrase "*exceeding strong*" being used to describe how things were going in Judah. Those are two very different phrases and levels! Because of sin, they deteriorated from "Things are going absolutely fantastic!" to "We're doing okay."

Okay, would actually be okay if one had never experienced "absolutely fantastic" and then deteriorated to the point of "okay."

DO refuse to be satisfied with "okay" in your spiritual life; "exceeding strong" is available if you will simply do right!

Personal Notes:

_____
_____
_____
_____
_____
_____
_____
_____
_____
_____
_____
_____
_____
_____
_____
_____
_____
_____
_____
_____
_____
_____
_____
_____
_____
_____
_____
_____
_____

Devotion 87

As 2 Chronicles 12 comes to an end, we are given a few verses summarizing the life and reign of Rehoboam.

2 Chronicles 12:13 *So king Rehoboam strengthened himself in Jerusalem, and reigned: for Rehoboam was one and forty years old when he began to reign, and he reigned seventeen years in Jerusalem, the city which the LORD had chosen out of all the tribes of Israel, to put his name there. And his mother's name was Naamah an Ammonitess.* **14** *And he did evil, because he prepared not his heart to seek the LORD.* **15** *Now the acts of Rehoboam, first and last, are they not written in the book of Shemaiah the prophet, and of Iddo the seer concerning genealogies? And there were wars between Rehoboam and Jeroboam continually.* **16** *And Rehoboam slept with his fathers, and was buried in the city of David: and Abijah his son reigned in his stead.*

There are two things exceedingly intriguing in this passage. The first is the identity of Rehoboam's mother: Naamah, who was an Ammonitess. One might think that identity as revealed here as a negative, but that does not at all seem to be the case. In fact, based on what Solomon wrote to his son in Proverbs 1:8 and 6:20 about obeying the law of his mother, Naamah seems, despite her background, to have been a good and godly influence!

But the second thing I notice is that Rehoboam did evil specifically because he did not prepare his heart to seek the LORD. Pay attention to that word "prepare," it makes all the difference in the world...

No one will ever accidentally seek the Lord and do right; that will always and only be an intentional thing. Nor does God "fling righteousness upon us unbeknownst to us." If we are going to do right, we MUST prepare our hearts, every single day, to seek the Lord. So DO each and every day intentionally set your mind and heart on the Lord, and seek Him out every moment of the day!

Personal Notes:

_____

_____

_____

_____

_____

_____

_____

_____

_____

_____

_____

_____

_____

_____

_____

_____

_____

_____

_____

_____

Devotion 88

As 2 Chronicles 13 begins Rehoboam is dead and Abijah, his son, is now on the throne. And the first thing on his mind was war.

2 Chronicles 13:1 *Now in the eighteenth year of king Jeroboam began Abijah to reign over Judah.* **2** *He reigned three years in Jerusalem. His mother's name also was Michaiah the daughter of Uriel of Gibeah. And there was war between Abijah and Jeroboam.* **3** *And Abijah set the battle in array with an army of valiant men of war, even four hundred thousand chosen men: Jeroboam also set the battle in array against him with eight hundred thousand chosen men, being mighty men of valour.*

As we begin to examine the numbers of this battle is clear that Abijah was at a two-to-one disadvantage. Not to get too far ahead of ourselves, but look down a few verses and notice how the battle went.

2 Chronicles 13:16 *And the children of Israel fled before Judah: and God delivered them into their hand.* **17** *And Abijah and his people slew them with a great slaughter: so there fell down slain of Israel five hundred thousand chosen men.*

God gave the victory, yes. And it is entirely appropriate for us to rejoice in any victory that God has given. And yet we must not miss the fact that half a million men lost their lives, a truly staggering number. Sons, fathers, brothers, husbands, half a million dead, never coming home. And it all started not with half a million, but with one man, Solomon, who rebelled against God in his latter years.

DO understand that one person's obedience can be the blessing and salvation of millions, while one person's disobedience can be the cursing and destruction of millions. So always DO right!

Personal Notes:

_____

_____

_____

_____

_____

_____

_____

_____

_____

_____

_____

_____

_____

_____

_____

_____

_____

_____

_____

_____

_____

_____

_____

Devotion 89

As we now begin to look at the details of the war between Abijah, the king of Judah, and Jeroboam the King of Israel, we find Abijah practically giving a sermon to his enemy before the fighting begins. But, like many careless sermons, it contained a mixture of truth and error.

2 Chronicles 13:4 *And Abijah stood up upon mount Zemaraim, which is in mount Ephraim, and said, Hear me, thou Jeroboam, and all Israel;* **5** *Ought ye not to know that the LORD God of Israel gave the kingdom over Israel to David for ever, even to him and to his sons by a covenant of salt?* **6** *Yet Jeroboam the son of Nebat, the servant of Solomon the son of David, is risen up, and hath rebelled against his lord.* **7** *And there are gathered unto him vain men, the children of Belial, and have strengthened themselves against Rehoboam the son of Solomon, when Rehoboam was young and tenderhearted, and could not withstand them.*

In case you have not recognized the error in this, pay attention to the phrase "Rehoboam was young and tenderhearted." That is how he described his father in reference to the split of the kingdom and his father's role in that split. But look back a few verses please into the previous chapter:

2 Chronicles 12:13 *So king Rehoboam strengthened himself in Jerusalem, and reigned: for Rehoboam was one and forty years old when he began to reign...*

The "young and tender" father he was talking about who blew the kingdom up with his rotten attitude was forty-one years old! Abijah was definitely playing fast and loose with the truth in that part of his message, which is what usually happens when one deviates from Scripture and starts preaching experience and preference.

As a child of God, whether you are a preacher or not, DO always tell the entire truth when you are supposedly speaking the Word of God; nothing else even remotely honors God appropriately!

Personal Notes:

_____

_____

_____

_____

_____

_____

_____

_____

_____

_____

_____

_____

_____

_____

_____

_____

_____

_____

_____

_____

Devotion 90

Abijah finally made it past the "error" part of the message and got down to some serious truth.

2 Chronicles 13:8 *And now ye think to withstand the kingdom of the LORD in the hand of the sons of David; and ye be a great multitude, and there are with you golden calves, which Jeroboam made you for gods.* **9** *Have ye not cast out the priests of the LORD, the sons of Aaron, and the Levites, and have made you priests after the manner of the nations of other lands? so that whosoever cometh to consecrate himself with a young bullock and seven rams, the same may be a priest of them that are no gods.* **10** *But as for us, the LORD is our God, and we have not forsaken him; and the priests, which minister unto the LORD, are the sons of Aaron, and the Levites wait upon their business:* **11** *And they burn unto the LORD every morning and every evening burnt sacrifices and sweet incense: the shewbread also set they in order upon the pure table; and the candlestick of gold with the lamps thereof, to burn every evening: for we keep the charge of the LORD our God; but ye have forsaken him.* **12** *And, behold, God himself is with us for our captain, and his priests with sounding trumpets to cry alarm against you. O children of Israel, fight ye not against the LORD God of your fathers; for ye shall not prosper.*

This truthful portion of Abijah's message can be summarized in two main points. Point one: you have forsaken God, gone into idolatry, kicked out God's men, and are wicked. Point two: we have not forsaken God, we have not gone into idolatry, we have not kicked out God's men, and we are righteous.

His conclusion could then be summarized this way, "Because of all this, you are going to lose."

That is a very personal and pointed message. And that is what made it such a good message! Speaking in vague generalities never really does anyone any good! As one old-time preacher quipped, "Some preachers have gotten to be experts at almost saying something!"

Truth ought to be clear, pointed, and applied. If it is not, DO look for a place where it is. And if it is, DO stick around and take it to heart!

Personal Notes:

_____

_____

_____

_____

_____

_____

_____

_____

_____

_____

_____

_____

_____

_____

_____

_____

_____

_____

_____

Devotion 91

We come now to an accounting of the battle between Abijah and Jeroboam:

2 Chronicles 13:13 *But Jeroboam caused an ambushment to come about behind them: so they were before Judah, and the ambushment was behind them.* **14** *And when Judah looked back, behold, the battle was before and behind: and they cried unto the LORD, and the priests sounded with the trumpets.* **15** *Then the men of Judah gave a shout: and as the men of Judah shouted, it came to pass, that God smote Jeroboam and all Israel before Abijah and Judah.* **16** *And the children of Israel fled before Judah: and God delivered them into their hand.* **17** *And Abijah and his people slew them with a great slaughter: so there fell down slain of Israel five hundred thousand chosen men.* **18** *Thus the children of Israel were brought under at that time, and the children of Judah prevailed, because they relied upon the LORD God of their fathers.*

Outnumbered two to one, outmaneuvered on the battlefield, there is no reason they should have won. And yet they did. And they did so specifically because "*they relied upon the LORD God of their fathers.*"

How old-fashioned! How quaint! And yet how effective every time it is tried. The account of Abijah in 1 Kings 15 tells us that he was not even a godly man! And yet in this one instance when he and the nation relied on God, God came through. And there was once a time when this other nation, America, understood that...

DO realize that America will never endure because of military or economic might. Pray for revival in this land, because only in relying on God will we ever know real peace and safety!

Personal Notes:

_____
_____
_____
_____
_____
_____
_____
_____
_____
_____
_____
_____
_____
_____
_____
_____
_____
_____
_____
_____
_____
_____
_____
_____
_____

Devotion 92

After old Solomon the womanizer, Rehoboam the jerk, and Abijah the wicked man who had exactly one godly moment, we finally come to a breath of fresh air named King Asa.

2 Chronicles 14:1 *So Abijah slept with his fathers, and they buried him in the city of David: and Asa his son reigned in his stead. In his days the land was quiet ten years.* **2** *And Asa did that which was good and right in the eyes of the LORD his God:* **3** *For he took away the altars of the strange gods, and the high places, and brake down the images, and cut down the groves:* **4** *And commanded Judah to seek the LORD God of their fathers, and to do the law and the commandment.* **5** *Also he took away out of all the cities of Judah the high places and the images: and the kingdom was quiet before him.* **6** *And he built fenced cities in Judah: for the land had rest, and he had no war in those years; because the LORD had given him rest.*

Verse two tells us that Asa "*did that which was good and right in the eyes of the LORD his God.*" That is why we find in verse one that "*In his days the land was quiet ten years,*" in verse five that "*the kingdom was quiet before him,*" and in verse six that "*the land had rest, and he had no war in those years; because the LORD had given him rest.*"

Peace and quiet all around... and all because he decided to do what was "*good and right in the eyes of the LORD.*"

If you want peace and rest and quiet, you could try emptying out your life savings and going on an around-the-world cruise. Or you could just always do whatever is good and right in the eyes of the LORD. Yes, sometimes trouble will find us even when we do right; but as a general truth, most of our trouble is self-inflicted and could be remedied just by putting aside our stubbornness and doing right! So, DO right!

Personal Notes:

_____

_____

_____

_____

_____

_____

_____

_____

_____

_____

_____

_____

_____

_____

_____

_____

_____

_____

_____

_____

Devotion 93

In our last devotion, we saw that God gave the land ten years of rest and quiet under King Asa. Historically, nations have tended to make the same mistake during times of peace, namely assuming that it will always be that way, and not making preparations in case it isn't. But King Asa did not make that mistake:

2 Chronicles 14:7 *Therefore he said unto Judah, Let us build these cities, and make about them walls, and towers, gates, and bars, while the land is yet before us; because we have sought the LORD our God, we have sought him, and he hath given us rest on every side. So they built and prospered. **8** And Asa had an army of men that bare targets and spears, out of Judah three hundred thousand; and out of Benjamin, that bare shields and drew bows, two hundred and fourscore thousand: all these were mighty men of valour.*

During the time of peace, King Asa built defensive walls, gates, towers, and bars around their cities. He also built up the military to 580,000 soldiers. It is likely that because it was such a very peaceful time there were some people complaining about all those efforts and expenditures, just like there would be among the leftists now. But look at the very next thing in the text:

2 Chronicles 14:9 *And there came out against them Zerah the Ethiopian with an host of a thousand thousand, and three hundred chariots; and came unto Mareshah.*

King Asa and Judah now found themselves unexpectedly facing a one-million-man army. And suddenly all of that preparation made sense...

Life has good days and bad days, peaceful days and tumultuous days. During the good and peaceful days, DO be actively preparing for the inevitable bad and tumultuous days. Trying to play "catch up" during the days of disaster is a disaster unto itself!

Personal Notes:

_____
_____
_____
_____
_____
_____
_____
_____
_____
_____
_____
_____
_____
_____
_____
_____
_____
_____
_____
_____
_____

Devotion 94

King Asa had prepared the land and the military as well as he could, and yet he was still outnumbered nearly two to one in the battle that thrust itself upon him. But Asa and Judah had something that their adversaries did not have; an active, vibrant relationship with the God of heaven. And that would make all the difference.

2 Chronicles 14:10 *Then Asa went out against him, and they set the battle in array in the valley of Zephathah at Mareshah. 11 And Asa cried unto the LORD his God, and said, LORD, it is nothing with thee to help, whether with many, or with them that have no power: help us, O LORD our God; for we rest on thee, and in thy name we go against this multitude. O LORD, thou art our God; let not man prevail against thee. 12 So the LORD smote the Ethiopians before Asa, and before Judah; and the Ethiopians fled. 13 And Asa and the people that were with him pursued them unto Gerar: and the Ethiopians were overthrown, that they could not recover themselves; for they were destroyed before the LORD, and before his host; and they carried away very much spoil.*

There is an interesting dynamic to take note of in this passage. King Asa prepared with all his might ahead of time... King Asa and his men went out to fight the battle... And yet he also said, "*Help us, O LORD our God; for we rest on thee, and in thy name we go against this multitude.*" This wise and godly king gave his best efforts both in preparing for the fight and in fighting the fight, and he also completely trusted the Lord for the victory. His trusting did not make him try any less, and his trying did not make him trust any less!

In everything you face in life, DO go all out both in trying and in trusting. Salvation has nothing to do with our works, but most everything else in life does!

Personal Notes:

_____

_____

_____

_____

_____

_____

_____

_____

_____

_____

_____

_____

_____

_____

_____

_____

_____

_____

_____

_____

_____

_____

Devotion 95

King Asa had just returned from his successful campaign against the attacking Ethiopians. And it was then that he was met by a prophet of God. Most of the time in the Old Testament when a prophet came out to speak to a king, it wasn't good. But in this case, it was.

2 Chronicles 15:1 *And the Spirit of God came upon Azariah the son of Oded: **2** And he went out to meet Asa, and said unto him, Hear ye me, Asa, and all Judah and Benjamin; The LORD is with you, while ye be with him; and if ye seek him, he will be found of you; but if ye forsake him, he will forsake you. **3** Now for a long season Israel hath been without the true God, and without a teaching priest, and without law. **4** But when they in their trouble did turn unto the LORD God of Israel, and sought him, he was found of them. **5** And in those times there was no peace to him that went out, nor to him that came in, but great vexations were upon all the inhabitants of the countries. **6** And nation was destroyed of nation, and city of city: for God did vex them with all adversity. **7** Be ye strong therefore, and let not your hands be weak: for your work shall be rewarded.*

Notice the doctrine of free will coursing through every one of these verses. Azariah made it clear that Asa and the kingdom had a choice either to seek God or forsake God and that God would respond accordingly. He concluded by saying, "*Be ye strong therefore, and let not your hands be weak: for your work shall be rewarded.*"

We do have actual choices to make every day of our lives. And every one of those choices will either be rewarded or punished, so always choose to DO right!

Personal Notes:

_____

_____

_____

_____

_____

_____

_____

_____

_____

_____

_____

_____

_____

_____

_____

_____

_____

_____

_____

_____

_____

_____

_____

_____

_____

_____

Devotion 96

Azariah's message to King Asa had its intended effect, a wonderful effect:

2 Chronicles 15:8 *And when Asa heard these words, and the prophecy of Oded the prophet, he took courage, and put away the abominable idols out of all the land of Judah and Benjamin, and out of the cities which he had taken from mount Ephraim, and renewed the altar of the LORD, that was before the porch of the LORD.* **9** *And he gathered all Judah and Benjamin, and the strangers with them out of Ephraim and Manasseh, and out of Simeon: for they fell to him out of Israel in abundance, when they saw that the LORD his God was with him.*

For all of his godliness and success, Asa had not yet removed the idols of the people from the land. But now, hearing the words of Azariah (here called Oded, letting us know that his father spoke them first), Asa became even more courageous in his doings for the Lord and removed them. He then renewed the altar of the Lord which had fallen into disrepair. But further down in the text we find an even more amazing item:

2 Chronicles 15:16 *And also concerning Maachah the mother of Asa the king, he removed her from being queen, because she had made an idol in a grove: and Asa cut down her idol, and stamped it, and burnt it at the brook Kidron.*

King Asa removed his own mother from her queenship because of her wickedness! When a person is willing to take God's side even over family, you know they are serious about walking with God!

DO be so serious about walking with God that you are even willing to stand against family if need be!

Personal Notes:

_____

_____

_____

_____

_____

_____

_____

_____

_____

_____

_____

_____

_____

_____

_____

_____

_____

_____

_____

_____

_____

_____

_____

_____

_____

Devotion 97

In his young and early years, King Asa showed both a firm commitment to righteousness and a firm trust that God would always take care of him and his people as he honored that commitment to righteousness. But like so many, something changed in his latter years.

2 Chronicles 16:1 *In the six and thirtieth year of the reign of Asa Baasha king of Israel came up against Judah, and built Ramah, to the intent that he might let none go out or come in to Asa king of Judah.* **2** *Then Asa brought out silver and gold out of the treasures of the house of the LORD and of the king's house, and sent to Benhadad king of Syria, that dwelt at Damascus, saying,* **3** *There is a league between me and thee, as there was between my father and thy father: behold, I have sent thee silver and gold; go, break thy league with Baasha king of Israel, that he may depart from me.*

Asa used both God's money and his own money to bribe a foreign king to protect him. And that lack of faith was not going to go unaddressed on God's part.

2 Chronicles 16:7 *And at that time Hanani the seer came to Asa king of Judah, and said unto him, Because thou hast relied on the king of Syria, and not relied on the LORD thy God, therefore is the host of the king of Syria escaped out of thine hand.* **8** *Were not the Ethiopians and the Lubims a huge host, with very many chariots and horsemen? yet, because thou* *didst rely on the LORD, he delivered them into thine hand.*

Hanani was absolutely right. King Asa once relied on God in a much bigger issue, and now could not bring himself to rely on God when facing a smaller foe. That inconsistency ended up costing him greatly.

DO actively remember all the great things God has ever done for you so that you will not forget to trust Him in other things, even smaller things, down the line!

Personal Notes:

_____

_____

_____

_____

_____

_____

_____

_____

_____

_____

_____

_____

_____

_____

_____

_____

_____

_____

Devotion 98

Hanani the prophet was still speaking to King Asa about his sinful lack of faith. And where the king had once welcomed the message of a prophet, Azariah, when it was a positive message, he reacted very differently to this negative message.

2 Chronicles 16:9 *For the eyes of the LORD run to and fro throughout the whole earth, to shew himself strong in the behalf of them whose heart is perfect toward him. Herein thou hast done foolishly: therefore from henceforth thou shalt have wars.* **10** *Then Asa was wroth with the seer, and put him in a prison house; for he was in a rage with him because of this thing. And Asa oppressed some of the people the same time.*

Wroth... in a rage... after being so humble in his early years King Asa finally reached a point where he felt like he no longer needed humility. He reached the horrible point of "how dare you question me." Not only did he not listen to the message of the prophet, he threw the prophet in prison, and then turned his rage on some of his own people and oppressed them.

Be careful never to get to the point where you cannot be corrected. If every message and every word has to be positive and uplifting, you have become a diva rather than a disciple. DO stay humble!

Personal Notes:

Devotion 99

We now come to the account of the end of King Asa, one of the very best of Judah's kings, yet a man who stumbled toward the end of his life.

2 Chronicles 16:11 *And, behold, the acts of Asa, first and last, lo, they are written in the book of the kings of Judah and Israel.* **12** *And Asa in the thirty and ninth year of his reign was diseased in his feet, until his disease was exceeding great: yet in his disease he sought not to the LORD, but to the physicians.* **13** *And Asa slept with his fathers, and died in the one and fortieth year of his reign.* **14** *And they buried him in his own sepulchres, which he had made for himself in the city of David, and laid him in the bed which was filled with sweet odours and divers kinds of spices prepared by the apothecaries' art: and they made a very great burning for him.*

In case you are wondering, there is nothing inherently sinful about doctors or medicine. One of the most precious people in the life of Paul the apostle was Luke the beloved physician! But Asa's disease in the feet is clearly tied by the context to his lack of faith and errors in judgment of his latter years. His physical problem was caused by a spiritual problem, and yet he sought for a medical answer when there is no medicine on earth that can fix such a thing.

DO allow God to get your attention when He is trying to do so; there isn't enough Tylenol on earth to make things better when you don't!

Personal Notes:

_____
_____
_____
_____
_____
_____
_____
_____
_____
_____
_____
_____
_____
_____
_____
_____
_____
_____
_____
_____
_____
_____
_____
_____
_____
_____
_____

Books in the Night Heroes Series

Cry From the Coal Mine (Vol. 1)
Free Fall (Vol. 2)
Broken Brotherhood (Vol. 3)
The Blade of Black Crow (Vol. 4)
Ghost Ship (Vol. 5)
When Serpents Rise (Vol. 6)
Moth Man (Vol. 7)
Runaway (Vol. 8)
Terror by Day (Vol. 9)
Winter Wolf (Vol. 10)

More Books by Dr. Bo Wagner

Beyond the Colored Coat
Don't Muzzle the Ox
From Footers to Finish Nails
I'm Saved! Now What???
Learning Not to Fear the Old Testament
Marriage Makers/Marriage Breakers

Daniel: Breathtaking
Esther: Five Feast and the Fingerprints of God
James: The Pen and the Plumb Line
Jonah: A Study in Greatness
Nehemiah: A Labor of Love
Romans: Salvation From A-Z
Ruth: Diamonds in the Darkness
Proverbs: Bright Lights from Dark Sayings Vol 1
Proverbs: Bright Lights from Dark Sayings Vol 2

Devotionals

DO Drops Volume 1
DO Drops Volume 2
DO Drops Volume 3
DO Drops Volume 4
DO Drops Volume 5
DO Drops Volume 6
DO Drops Volume 7

Sci-Fi

Zak Blue and the Great Space Chase Series:
Falcon Wing (Vol. 1)
Enter the Maelstrom (Vol. 2)

www.ingramcontent.com/pod-product-compliance
Lightning Source LLC
Chambersburg PA
CBHW060155070426
42447CB00033B/1421